HIGHER THOUGHTS

(How to Upgrade the Brain Biblically)

M.I. Bello

Copyright ©2017 **M.I. Bello**

ISBN: 978-978-54741-9-0

All rights reserved.
No part of this book may be reproduced, distributed, stored in a retrieval system or transmitted, in any form or by any means, electronic, electrostatic, magnetic tape, mechanical, photocopying, recording or otherwise without prior written permission from the Publisher. For information about permission to reproduce selections from this book, write to info@wrr.ng.

National Library of Nigeria Cataloguing-in-Publication Data

Printed and Published in Nigeria by:
Words Rhymes & Rhythm Limited
Suite C309, Global Plaza Plot 366, Obafemi Awolowo Way, Jabi District, Abuja, Nigeria.
08169027757, 08060109295
www.wrr.ng

Contents

INTRODUCTION 4

CHAPTER ONE: THE BRAIN WORLD 11

CHAPTER TWO: INTELLIGENCE 19

CHAPTER THREE: PSYCHOLOGY OF WEALTH 31

CHAPTER FOUR: HIGHER THOUGHTS........................52

CHAPTER FIVE: BRAIN UPGRADE 64

CHAPTER SIX: GENIUS 117

CHAPTER SEVEN: HEAD ATTACKERS......................123

REFERENCES 135

INTRODUCTION

Looking gloomy, my friend walked up to me, he put out what seems to be a paper from his trouser back pocket. He pointed it towards me and exclaimed, "It has happened again."

Relinquishing my hopes of getting a nap and myself also reluctant to collect his paper, I asked, "What do you mean?"

He said, "This is the second time I am staying an extra year in college and each time I tried so hard and light seemed to shine at the tunnel end or should I say 'probably was about having a jail break'. I assume doing well in the exams, but when the results are out, I get the worst news of my life."

"Oh! I am a failure," he concluded. While I ran across the "encourage dictionary" in my head to find words that could calm him down. He continued, "What makes me different from those that are tagged brilliant? I cannot do it anymore, I think I will..." he said. The rest of the story is reserved.

The question of "what makes me different" that my friend was asking is the question many others experiencing similar issues whether in career, business, education or any life endeavour are asking also. Some however resorted to asking counsellors and psychologists. Many literatures, researches, articles and practical guides in the market have tried providing listed habits, attitudes and practices that are thought to be responsible for the "differences in men" in the context of achieving success and excellence. It is not that these already available books, articles and researches are not helpful. Millions of people have contacted these "writings", thousands who have been motivated to success by application of these highlighted principles. Thousands however remain "failures" or mostly staying at "status-quo" level. The problem is that we have overlooked a fundamental truth: people have different brain power.

In the case of Abel, a childhood friend of mine, who started off a sales business for two years now, I visited him one day and asked how his business was faring. Abel looked at me as though reminded of a tragic event when he heard me say, "How is your sales business doing now?" He hissed and sadly said, "It is not working at all. Things are stagnant, or should I blame it on the economy. I then said to him, "You started your sales business two years ago, you may however be operating like a novice. Have you tried reading Brian Tracy's book on "psychology of selling"? It is really going to help.". You can add to that other great literatures on success in business and financial..." Abel lifted up his head expressing tiredness of hearing the same old suggestions. He interrupted and said, "I have read and applied all the success strategy principles or whatsoever have come my way. It is yet not working."

Abel, now 29 years in age sat two years back with me on a transport bus. He explained to me, his frustrations with college life, his decisions to drop out of college, and to invest in a sales business with his savings of long engaged restaurant part-time job.

Abel has had poor performances in the past years in college and had to stay some extra years in a class. I replied him, "No, don't do that, even with your business dreams, education is very important in this 21st century."

"Ah!" Shouted Abel, he laughed and said, "Remember, most great men and entrepreneurs were college dropout; Mark Zuckerberg, Bill Gates..." he continued with an unending list of names.

Two years have passed already; he is struggling and experiencing regrets in business too.

Napoleon Hill wrote, "Think and Grow Rich". Tom Corley wrote "Rich Habits: Secret of Success of Wealthy People". However, whether 'thoughts, actions, decisions, habits, mindsets, creativity, innovations, paradigms, intelligence, ideas, coordination or knowledge', they are all imbedded in the brain. Most motivational and wealth creation writers conclusively suggest "thoughts" (positive) as a major factor to the creation of success and wealth. Nevertheless, consider this; although millions of such writings as "think and grow rich" have been read by millions of people, many who have been motivated to becoming self-made millionaires, others however still remain where they were after contact with such book, or at least improved a bit, because they are left still with the responsibility to think for their own selves to creating their own productivity. What we do not consider is that the thinking, thinking pattern and thinking productivity of some people differ from others. This is where brain power comes to play. Our brain power determines how productive our thinking can be to birth ideas before other factors as decisions, actions, attitude could drive to it final end product: success, productivity or excellence.

Habits: (emotionalized thoughts and repeated actions), especially those regarded as "success-habits" or positive habits have been studied and concluded on to prompt success and productivity also, probably to most people who practise them. However, I have never come across hundred percent testimonies or assurance that if assuming a hundred people practised such habits in a range of time allowable, they all hundred will become successful. So what is the cause of this inequality in the practised habit to translate into a wealthy physical reality? One, which is top on the list, is the fact that not all brains equally having knowledge of these value-driven habits are able to equally translate or express them consistently until their physical reality alters. Their inconsistency and low expression power may be due to forgetfulness, low endurance, low stamina, brain dullness, low intelligence quotient (IQ) or negative mental attitudes, all which are fishes that swim in the ocean of their brain.

For Shiv Khera in "you can win" highlighted attitude as a factor to success. He said that "our attitude determines how we look at set back". To have a positive attitude, it can be a stepping stone to success. A negative attitude can be a stumbling block. He went ahead to also say that "great organisations are not measured by pay and working conditions but by attitudes and relationships." But attitude (positive) towards a challenge, task, job, satisfying a market demand, being a top sales person, excelling in academics are enhanced by the feeling of self competence, confidence, and positive self concept prompted also by skilfulness, adequate competitive knowledge and excellence in what you do. These skills, knowledge and your differing ingredient that add to your specialness are determined by your brain power.

Brain upgrade is not just about possessing high intelligence. Shiv Khera said there are many walking encyclopaedias that are failures. Very true! Brain upgrade has to do with a whole lot of things; competence, common sense, good judgement, attitude, courage, desire, focus, commitment, creativity, intelligence, skill, productive planning, productive goal settings, which are all build-ups of the mind and brain.

Intelligence is quickness to learn and think, ability is the skill to apply thoughts and knowledge, competence is the desire and ability to apply what is learned to productiveness. Desire is the attitude that makes a skilful person competent. These qualities are all encompassing and dependent on each other to make a better man. Brain upgrade is the upgrade of these qualities in man.

Another motivational writer said "there is a direct correlation between motivation and productivity. On an organisational level, he gave an example that people who do just enough to get by so they don't get fired will never be reliable to any organisation.

Inspiration is the mother of motivation. Inspiration is changed thinking while motivation is changed action. But know this, no matter how you try to inspire some people to motivation, it becomes a fruitless effort, reasons be that their brain might be un- upgraded, may be dull, inactive, passive, slow to motivation and unable to cross the inspiration to motivation line.

Upgraded brains picture and desire a good life, a better one. It desires to do the right things for the right reasons and that what makes a difference. Shiv Khera shared a story in his book "you can win" of two brothers. One was a drug addict and a drunk who often harassed his family. The other brother was a very successful businessman, respected in society and had a wonderful family. Some people wanted to find out why two brothers from the same parents, brought up in the same family and circumstances could be so different.

The first one was asked, *"how come you do what you do? You are a drug addict, a drunk, and you often harass your family. What motivates you? He said, my father. They asked, what about him? The reply was, my father was a drug addict, a drunkard and he too harasses his family. What do you expect me to be? That is what I am, I took it from him.* They went to the brother who was doing alright and asked him the same question. *"How comes you are doing the right things and also successful? What is your source of motivation? He said: my father, when I was a little boy; I used to see my dad drunk and doing all the wrong things. I made up my mind that that is not what I wanted to be"*. Both were deriving their motivation from the same source, but one was using it positively and the other negatively.

The cause of the differing use of same motivation source is highly likely to be the brain factor. The positive business man had a brain that pictured and desired a better life, so irrespective of his environmental influence and reality, his motivation was geared towards an already programmed brain target: (better life) – the power of an upgraded brain.

The brain becomes therefore not only the most important but most wanted part of man. It controls body functioning, determines ones creativity, intelligence, attitude, motivation, productivity and money. The brain has been responsible for the Nobel Prize winnings of its winners, whether in science, art and technology. The brain is responsible for the success of many great achievers. The brain makes the best. The brain initiates all forms of prowess and skill in music, arts, literature writings, fashion and entertainments.

The brain is the centre of intelligence. The brain is the power of wealth creation. It is the coordinating centre of the body. We can therefore conclude that the brain is the greatest asset of man. Change your brain, change your life. Upgrade your brain, upgrade your life.

CHAPTER ONE: THE BRAIN WORLD

The brain located in the head is the most complex of all body organs. In a human, the cerebral cortex contains approximately 25-35 billion neurons. They are connected by synapses to several thousand other neurons. Axons are fibre-like communication link between neurons and carried trains of signal to different parts of the brain and body recipient cell. It is a three-pound organ, it is the centre of intelligence, body coordinating centre, interpreter of the senses, initiator of body movement, and controller of behaviour. The brain is the source of all the qualities that define our humanity. The brain has been a fascinating subject to philosophers and science researchers for centuries but it has begun to unfold overtime, due to the great pace of research in neurological and behavioural sciences, and this has helped us understand the science of the brain clearly. The brain is like a processing system. All its parts work together, but each part has its own special properties.

In the case of our own study, otherwise, the forebrain, mid and hind brain divides the brain into the three basic unit, we shall separate the brain into two parts basically.

1. Hindbrain
2. Forebrain

The hindbrain consists of the upper spinal cord, the brain stem and the cerebellum. The brain stem, sometimes referred to as the reptilian brain is primarily made up of medulla oblongata, the Pons and the midbrain. The brain stem controls all autonomic process and ensures our survival. It controls respiration heart rate, swallowing and organ function. It prompts hunger, sex drive, and the fight/flight mechanism, the cerebellum coordinates movement and is involved in learned rote movement. The cerebellum enables the playing of piano, drums, swimming or hitting a tennis ball.

The midbrain is the uppermost part of the brainstem. It controls some reflex actions, part of the control circuit for eye movements and other voluntary movements. The hindbrain therefore has to do with body functioning, autonomic movements, reflex actions and some voluntary movement.

The forebrain is the upgradeable part of the brain, highly developed and largest part of the human brain. We shall separate it into:

    a. Neocortex
    b. Limbic system

Limbic system is located deep within the brain, close to the inner wall of each cerebral hemisphere. It can be called emotional brain.

These structures determine our emotional state and even modify our perceptions and responses depending on that state, and allow us to initiate movements without thinking about them. The limbic system takes part in memory storage, both long term and short term. It consist of

    a. Hypothalamus; controls appetite, hormones and body temperature.
    b. Thalamus; affects touch, pain, temperature and muscles.

c. Hippocampus; where short term memory is stored; controls speaking also.
d. Olfactory lobe; triggers smell but is greatly reduced in humans and other primates (whose senses are dominated by information acquired by sight rather than smell).
e. Cingulated cortex; it is involved in developing new skills and for survival by creating mirror neurons,
f. Reticular activating system; check-up, allows or blocks the sensory information we take in.
g. Basal ganglia; are a group of interconnected structures in the forebrain. This is where habits are stored and decision made. The basal ganglia acts like the port of an electronic device e.g. mobile phone for neural pathway created in the neocortex. Habits are formed when there are repeated uses of certain neural pathways. The brain will create a port inside the basal ganglia and link to that often used neural path. That created port can stay there forever. That is why habits are not easily broken. According to Tom Corley, it takes 18 to 254 days for the brain to create a port in the basal ganglia and thus form a habit.

Neocortex; may be referred to as the higher brain, cerebrum or cerebral cortex. It sits at the topmost part of the brain. It is the source of intellectual activities, it is responsible for thought creation, learning, long-term memory, decision making, planning and imagination. It allows you to recognize people, read books, and play games. The neocortex (cerebrum) is the most part of the brain, it splits into two halves by a deep fissure, but communicate with each other through a thick tract of nerve fibres at the base of this fissure. The two halves of the cerebrum are mirror images of each other but play different roles. For instance, the right hemisphere seems to control many abstract reasoning skills, while the ability to form words seems to lie primarily in the left hemisphere.

PLACE OF THOUGHT

Both separate cerebral hemispheres can be divided into lobes, each with its speciality and function. The cerebral hemisphere has two frontal lobes lying behind the fore head directly. The frontal lobes are activated when imagining, during reasoning or planning a schedule. One of the ways the frontal lobes seems to do these things is by acting as short term storage sites, allowing one idea to be kept in mind while other ideas are considered. Both frontal lobes have a motor which helps to control voluntary movement. In a portion of the left frontal lobe is the broca's area allowing thoughts to be transformed to words.

The parietal lobes are paired lobes located behind the frontal lobes; they are focused on taste, aroma and food texture. They have a sensory area just behind the motor area which receives information about taste, touch, and temperature and body movement. The occipital lobe located at the back of the brain processes images from the eyes and link that information with images stored in memory. They also capture printed words and enhance their understanding.

Temporal lobes are the last lobes of the cerebral hemisphere. They lie directly under the parietal lobe. They are responsible for receiving information from the ears, forming and retrieving memories, including those associated with music and words. They also seem to integrate memories and sensation of taste, sound, sight and touch.

Most of the actual information processing in the brain takes place in the cerebral cortex. The cortex is a thick layer of tissue coating the surface of the cerebrum and (cerebellum). The folds in the brain add to the brain surface area and therefore increase the amount of gray matter and quantity of information that can be processed.

THOUGHT-TO-ATTITUDE CHAIN

A thought or action coupled with any powerful emotion such as desire, focus, drive or more creates automatically a neural pathway in the brain which is stored permanently into our long term memory. These emotionalized thoughts or actions already stored acts like software programming in our cerebral cortex or neocortex. When this emotionalized thoughts or action are repeated over and over again, the cerebral neural pathway in the cerebral cortex then creates what is the equivalent of a neural wire (like a wire connected to a mobile phone). The neural pathway, by virtue of this neural wire is then linked to a newly formed neural port (like the port of a device) in the basal ganglia. The repeated emotionalized thoughts or actions, eventually become habit by reprogramming our minds and foundation of our belief system. If a "belief" is programmed or created, that programming sticks and will direct our attitude and behaviour in such a way as to ensure the "belief" are actualized. Repeating behaviour or repeating expression of an attitude still eventually becomes a habit. If that behaviour is good, such as commitment to reading, it stays and the effect is self improvement that can lead to better productivity or maybe you have developed a better relationship with your business consumers, then higher sales. If that behaviour is bad, such as overeating, it also sticks and the effect is obesity leading to heart disease, or any other detrimental health issues.

GOOD NEWS – BAD NEWS – GOOD NEWS

In context of productivity, good news is that our belief system can be reprogrammed through this same process. If we change our repetitive emotionalized thoughts or actions and repeating them over and over again, they will eventually become habits which will alter our behaviour and attitude. Productive and successful people reprogram their minds for success and productivity by practising productive thinking, actions and habits.

A bad news is this; *man without the brain cannot produce thoughts.*

Thomas and Os, two men of the same business kind and manner of operation, even with the same annual profit went to a business seminar organised by top sales professionals in their city. They were given guides to ideas they could think of, create and increase their business sales. After three months, Mr. Os had caught an idea, modified his business operative methods and his sales went up twice high. On the other hand, Mr. Thomas struggled with getting or creating an idea, implementing new change and records of his sales remained unchanged

Man cannot produce "productive thoughts" at his own will. The neocortex of the brain produces such thought for him when trained to, which if not discarded will be stored in the long term memory. These thoughts will end up in the basal ganglia where habits are formed. Upgraded brains have been proven to produce more productive thoughts faster and easier than other brains less upgraded. The degree of upgrade of the brain determines the productiveness of our thoughts and well being

Another good news is that brains can be upgraded at any level by using a number of scientific and biblical proven tools and strategies.

MOTIVATION

Individuals and their brain are programmed genetically to behave in ways that ensure their survival. In the context of productivity and human survival, the brain provides surviving and or productive goals which translate into a set of specific surviving-promoting and or productive-promoting behaviours such as desire for love, satisfaction, food, esteem etc. The motivational system in the brain monitors the state of satisfaction for these goals, and activates behaviours to meet any need that arises. Berridge K.C in "motivation concepts in behavioural neuroscience" said that the motivational system in the brain works largely by a reward-punishment mechanism. When a particular behaviour is followed by favourable results, the reward mechanism in the brain is activated, which induces structural processes inside the brain that cause the same behaviour to be repeated later, whenever a similar situation arise. Conversely, when behaviour is followed by unfavourable consequences, the brain's punishment mechanism is activated inducing structural process that causes the behaviour to be suppressed when similar situation arises in the future.

MEMORY

Individuals encode, store and retrieve information from the memory. Personal and life experiences can also be kept in memory. Whenever people successfully recall a prior experience, they must have encoded, stored and retrieved information about the experience. Humans and their brains are capable of modifying their behaviour as a result of experience. Because behaviour is driven by brain activity, changes in behaviour must somehow correspond to changes inside the brain.

Memory and learning are closely related. In fact, psychologists often refer to the learning – memory process as a means of incorporating all facets of encoding, storage and retrieval. Whereas learning is often used to refer to processes involved in the initial acquisition or encoding of information, memory more often refers to later storage and retrieval of information.

CHAPTER TWO: INTELLIGENCE

Sir Frances Galton was a British scientist. He pioneered a study in the later decades of the 1800's to measure difference in individual mental ability and also sensitivity to the environment. He compared the accomplishment of people from different ancestry of prominent English families. He evaluated each of his subjects on their fames as supposed by honours, awards, recognitions and encyclopaedia entries. He concluded that the "accomplishment-mark" he measured ran in families and is derived from a hereditary factor. What Sir Galton did not consider is the place of environmental and social interaction in intelligence development. Since his subjects were from prominent families, it is highly likely that a better environment and social interactions helped upgrade their intelligences faster than those from the average or poor families.

The influence of hereditary factor on intelligence is tangible, maybe strong. However not solemnly by it alone, because there are cases of even identical twins possessing different level of intelligence. However, the truth which is our most interest, is that intelligence (productive thinking) can improve irrespective of whether ones progenitors were of low or high IQ

Good news! Over the years, environmental factors comprising surrounding external influences including education, food, cultural information and social exposure have been considered now to account for between 30 and 60 percent of total variation in human intelligence. However, in a study case, likewise in many others, of an identical twins of both 9 years of age, Lucy and Beatrice who were from same rich English family and were to take intelligence test for admission into secondary school. Beatrice was good with the piano, so to say; she was real good for her age limit. Lucy on other hand spent a deal of time reading and seems to be better in science. After undergoing the same Lewis Terman IQ test, Beatrice barely scored a 9 mental age, therefore was assigned an IQ score of 100 while Lucy scored a mental age of 12 therefore an IQ of 130. That is to say, Lucy, 9 years old could solve problem or think as a 12 years old should properly do. She had higher intelligence than Beatrice, her twin. Both of them were from the same family or race, same sex, same progenitor, same environment, and same social exposure. It won't be wrong then to ask why the variation in their mental age?

It may likely be that other factors that have prompted upgrade to Lucy's intelligence might have not been considered. The brain is the centre of intelligence, and intelligence is the root and fruit of productive thinking. Intelligence is not the secret of success and wealth solemnly, but a great factor involved in the success of many personalities and the backbone of industrialisation, scientific and technological development.

Intelligence has a wide array of definitions:
- Ability to learn and comprehend.
- Ability to practically and effectively apply a known fact.
- Ability to solve problems.

- Ability to reason, judge and understand properly.
- Ability to possess creativity and interpersonal skills.
- Ability to communicate effectively
- Ability to think rationally and act purposefully.
- Ability to plan and pursue a goal.
- General cognitive ability.

Intelligence is the lead difference between a successful entrepreneur, politician, or student and the strugglers. It is the difference between distinction and average; it is what stands out the Nobel Prize winners, scientists and economists. It gives birth to outstanding researchers, innovators, great artist, musicians, scholars and some other multibillionaire entrepreneurs.

Different individuals have different levels of intelligence. We know this because intelligence can actually be quantified or measured especially in younger people. Although, the standard test to measure intelligence has been argued by a number of theorists to measure only a portion of human abilities but others believe that such test measures total intelligence accurately and that, its measurement cannot be invalidated by the lack of agreement on a particular definition of intelligence since different scholars have different opinions and views to the meaning of intelligence. However, whether this measurement quantifies or defines intelligence or part of it, it has been able to point out people who have higher intelligence level than others.

There are many tests to measure intelligence, but we would take interest in the IQ: intelligence Quotient, which has been proven reliable to measure intelligence in children, but might not do well in adults because intelligence levels off in adults: cognitive mechanics as ability to reason abstractly, recall fast, processing speed, visual memory, motor memory, processing accuracy (those with a genetic foundation) decline during aging whereas cognitive qualities or pragmatics obtained through experience such as skills of profession, reading, writing, speaking, language comprehension remain or increase with age.

Intelligence Quotient (IQ) measures level of intelligence taking into account a child's mental age and chronological age. Individuals whose mental and chronological age equals will have an average IQ (specifically 100) reason be that chronological age defines the individual actual age while mental age define the typical intelligence level for a particular age

Intelligence quotient (IQ) = mental age/ chronological age x 100

Remember the story of Lucy and Beatrice, Lucy had an IQ score that equals 130 (above average IQ), meaning her mental age exceeds her chronological age. For Beatrice, she reasons, thinks and act like a proper 9 years old, therefore assigned an average IQ.

The distribution of intelligence (Stanford IQ) gives ten intelligence levels in men. The average intelligence which ranges between 90 to109 is the middle score range that most men falls into. The excellent book "an enemy called average" by John mason attempts to teach how to push above the average life because a greater percentage of humanity lives and act at the survival or average level. So is the case of intelligence in humans.

Most men are average because their IQs are average. Most people never think nor dream big because their IQs swing within the average. The medicine for an average and low IQ is the brain upgrade.

The ten IQ levels according to the Binet distribution of intelligence are;

- Very superior intelligence (outstanding, gifted); above 130 IQ score
- Superior intelligence (excellence, capable); 120 to 129 IQ score
- High average intelligence (good, able): 110 to 119 score
- Average intelligence (average, general): 90 to 109 score
- Low average intelligence (middle class): 80 to 89 score
- Borderline intellectual functioning (strugglers, low): 71 to 79 score
- Mild mental retardation (poor): 55 to 79 score
- Moderate retardation (very poor): 40 to 54 score
- Severe mental retardation (extremely poor): 25 to 39 score
- Profound mental retardation (bad): below 25 score.

For the determinate or influencing factors affecting intelligence, there is an ancient theory which says that everyone is born with a fixed amount of intelligence that cannot be lessen or improved upon. This fixed intelligence argued by the theory is determined by genetics only. Overtime, almost all scientists have come to agree that environmental factors, sex, racial and ethnical difference, and not genetics alone have also a very good hand influencing intelligence. Other researches in very recent times have tried to debate the cause of average IQ variation around the world. Few among the arguers are Niegel Barber who says variation in IQ is due primarily to difference in education. Donald Templer and Hiroko Arikawa argued that colder climates are difficult to live in such that evolution favours higher IQ in people that live in those areas.

A study by Christopher Hassal and Thomas Sherratt supported with a study by Christopher Eppig, Correy Fincher and Randy Thornhill concluded that there is a strong relationship between levels of infectious disease and IQ and that infectious disease may be the cause of global variation in human intelligence. In their view, exposure to infectious disease during childhood may likely rob large amount of energy from a developing brain and cause low IQ.

Intelligence improves, upon brain upgrade not regarding one's intelligence level or score or factors (environment, genetic, race, sex, climate, evolution, or disease) that are the lead cause for such level. The advantages or profit of possessing high intelligence to any man is enviable as it can prompt the following to happen:

- Academic excellence
- Professional excellence
- Good job opportunities
- Good self esteem
- Self confidence
- Quickness to learn new things
- Quickness to solve and adapt to new challenges.
- Award winner

- Promotion/ recognition
- Positive self concept

Intelligence however should never be alluded as the only key to success. Infact, intelligence plays less than half the role in the making of successful and wealthy individuals. Shiv Khera in his book "you can win" went as far as to say that "a person can and will be successful with or without formal education, if they have 5c's; character, commitment, conviction, courtesy, and courage which are still products of brain upgrade. So brain upgrade goes beyond upgrading and improving on intelligence. It is upgrading all brain activities until it pushes to better productivity.

What brain activities?

Intelligence
Thoughts
Habits
Imagination
Behaviour
Attitude
Motivations
Memory
Cognitions
State of mind/ mindsets
State of being
Body internal environment (control)

INTELLIGENCE AND THOUGHTS

Intelligence is the product and root of productive thinking. A person is considered intelligent, if his thoughts are productive (effectively able to recall and or apply already stored information: process data to become information that can profit self and humanity).

Great effort, on the other hand, spent on thinking productively builds up intelligence. It is called the intelligence–thought cycle.

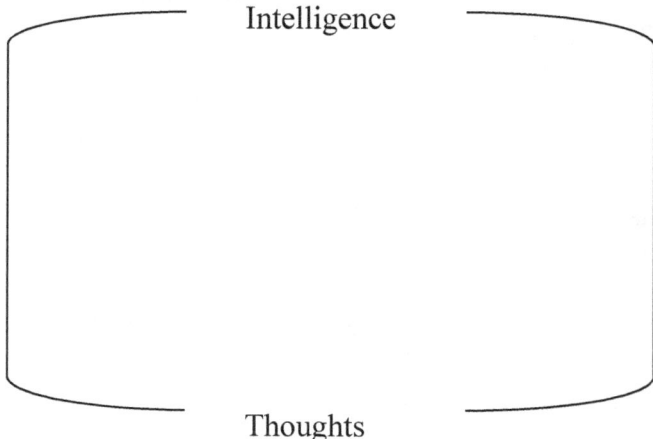

I.T CYCLE

THOUGHTS
The word "thought" comes from "pencan", meaning to "consider of in the mind" or to "consider". There are no general agreement to the meaning of thought and its creation process even though it is a basic human activity but can maybe referred to forms, ideas, notions, hunches that results from thinking.

Thinking allows us to make meaning of, perceive, know, interpret, or model the environment and the world we experience. The word "thought" may mean differently in other forms and contexts;

An idea, interpretation, recollection, intention, anticipation, belief/opinion, reasoning, consideration, mental activity, contemplation, evaluation, planning, remembrance etc.

Higher Thoughts

Thoughts are qualities that define a person. There is a direct relationship between one's persistent thoughts and what he becomes in life. Thoughts can translate, or fully express itself into physical reality when it manifests into habits, alters attitudes and behaviours consequently affecting one's life totally.

Humanity (man) engages in various kinds of thought/thinking pattern, a few among which include;

- *Routine thoughts*: thoughts on how to run our daily lives and activities. Plan the day and pursue daily set goals. Example:
  Thoughts on what to eat
  Thoughts on when to sleep
  Thoughts of what to buy
  Thoughts of how to get to work
- *Right thoughts*: these are generally accepted, good and right ways of thinking on what to do and how to do it in the way beneficial to man and his environment.
- *Bad thoughts*; these are products of wrong thinking that are not generally accepted to man and his environment.
- *Mediocre thoughts:* unproductive thoughts, loser mentality; these are thoughts that are generally not constructive, unproductive and do not have a good esteem or exceptions of what they can do.
- *Pure thoughts:* these are thoughts that can actually brighten the mind and beautify the character of a man. These are generally accepted thoughts in the concept of godliness. Pure thoughts can broadly entail righteous thoughts,

godly thoughts, honest thoughts, holy thoughts, just thoughts and virtuous thoughts etc.
- *Strange thoughts*: these are thoughts that are unusual, odd and naturally abnormal to the human mind. Example; suicidal thoughts, perverse thoughts, wicked thoughts etc.
- *Troubled thoughts:* these are thoughts of unrest, uncertainty, insecurity and fear.
- *Proud thoughts*: over raiding; thoughts that view or esteem oneself above others. Beneath these thought kinds are;
  Arrogant thoughts: thoughts that translate into harsh words and arrogant behaviours.
  Critical thoughts: thoughts that translate into opinions harshly expressed.
- *Intelligent thoughts:* these are thoughts that stem from possessing a high IQ or mental activity. These thoughts enable us to;
  a. Solve mathematical and scientific problems
  b. Apply and interpret properly grammatical situations
  c. Deal with complex intellectual ideas
- *Stronghold thoughts;* these are perpetual thought state resulting in alteration of one's habitual behaviour and character. These thought types are usually difficult to alter.
- *Carnal thoughts;* these are thoughts relating to improper desire and appetite for;
  a. Sex
  b. Sexual appeal
  c. Arousing actions and words
  d. Sometimes, excessive obsessions for food and money

- *Traumatizing thoughts*: they usually come from recollection of past or immediate tragic or traumatizing experiences, occurrences, regrets, lose or separation.
- *Spiritual thoughts:* these are thoughts that arise by involvement in spiritual or religious activities:
    a. Meditation
    b. Prayer
    c. Hypnosis
    d. Spiritual ecstasy

These thoughts are the product of the makeup of the mind and brain feed from any of the following:
   a. Experiences
   b. Environment
   c. Education
   d. Cultural information
   e. Religious belief
   f. Motivations (personal achievements, envy, lust, gossips, fear etc.)
   g. Social interactions/association
   h. Orientations
   i. Occurrences/events/exposures

There are many other kinds of thought dominating the brain of the natural man, other than those enlisted above. But in order to achieve a purpose of this book (positioning the brain for better productivity, success and wealth through productive thinking and habits), we shall look at two kinds of thoughts of which every man should certainly fall beneath one. These thoughts have been able to separate the poor and the rich, they define success and failure, and they determine productivity and un-productivity.

1. ***Higher thoughts:*** could mean many things both in the context of intelligence and prosperity. They could mean the following;
   a. Rich thoughts
   b. Positive thoughts
   c. Rich ideas
   d. Success thoughts
   e. Creative thoughts

   Wealthy and successful people invest a great deal to take care of their "minds" to engage it in rich, positive or high thinking always. These thoughts would then translate into rich habitual behaviour by creating a permanent neural pathway from the neocortex (place of thought creation) to the basal ganglia (habit formation site) in the brain. These rich habits which actually require little brain processing power as thought initiation easily pushes them into activities that increase their success and wealth potentials or index.

2. **Baseline thoughts**: relate to the thinking pattern of most poor and average people. These thoughts are responsible for the poverty habits and detrimental behaviours that accumulate debts and bring lack. This phase "baseline thoughts" could be used contextually differently in the school of prosperity;
   a. Mediocre thoughts
   b. Poverty thoughts
   c. Unproductive thoughts
   d. Uncreative thoughts
   e. Lack of intelligence.
   f. Foolish thinking

CHAPTER THREE: PSYCHOLOGY OF WEALTH

It is important to note the limitation of intelligence especially in the world of financial freedom, because the author's desire is not only to increase the intelligence index of the readers but also to psychologically bring them to the place of wealth.

Psychological wealth has a long existing track record of translating into physical wealth. The contending issue becomes how one gets psychologically wealthy and even if the process is understood properly, how does the brain becomes receptive to such processes? These will be understood as you continue reading this book.

Financial freedom is the desire of every natural man. The journey to this freedom begins however from the brain and the reason for the unveiling of the subject of financial freedom by the writer is to bring to the reader's awareness the awesomeness and great potentials of the brain and therefore how it becomes increasingly important for them to continually engage in brain upgrading.

In the world of financial freedom, there are many laws, however one is fundamental, dominating, unknown to many, yet grants access. This law is known as the law of reality which sets out to explain that or how financial fortune or poverty is dependent directly on a person's persistent thought (thought pattern, mindset and paradigm).

This law then divides individuals into two major classes:
    a. People with poor thoughts (poor thinking pattern, poor mindset).

b. People with wealthy thoughts (wealthy thought pattern, wealthy mindset).

Every process that may lead to financial fortunes, whether habits, attitude, motivations begins with the conceiving (of thoughts). The connection and translation process between thoughts and these processes have been explained in preceding chapters.

It is clear as established by experts like Remez Sasson, Ayn Rand, and Tom Corley that wealth creation and financial freedom require both thoughts and physical actions, even if thoughts remain the initial step. And although thoughts without physical action is useless day dreaming, actions itself can never be taken expect based on rational thoughts.

The fact that thoughts determine wealth can be or is proven through the watch of history and the emergence of modernity. In past ages or centuries, poverty rate amongst people and societies were high, innovations were scarce, standard of living for many was porous and there was much less wealth per person. This was because the mind of men of those ages were un-enlightened, creatively unimaginative, inactive and little able to think much. Overtime, human thoughts created new technologies, innovations, discoveries that enabled unprecedented per capital wealth creation by being much more productive in labour.

An expert made this known fact "the explosive upward growth of real income for average American workers in the nineteenth and twentieth century was made possible by the explosion in thought that happened in the renaissance, enlightenment and the industrial revolution."

Human thought therefore remain the root of financial freedom or poverty

What is financial freedom? It means;
   a. Attaining freedom from lack and poverty.
   b. Attaining freedom from financial insufficiency.
   c. Freedom from the effects of lack, poverty and insufficiency.
   d. Abundant financial supplies and resources.
   e. Ability to possess resources that can replenish, multiply, and sustain financial supplies.

Negative effects of lack and poverty
   a. Insecurity
   b. Fear
   c. Abuse (physical, mental and social)
   d. Greed/envy/bitterness
   e. Social vices etc.

On the opposite, poverty means a state of perpetual lack and insufficiency of financial resources often characterized by lack of productivity.

If thoughts could be responsible for these financial fortune or lack, there must be thoughts pattern known for creating wealth and thought pattern that leads to poverty.

THOUGHT PATTERN THAT LEADS TO POVERTY:

These are thoughts, mindset, and paradigms that have kept poor those people who embrace them, some of these patterns of thought may include;
   a. Thoughts that money and abundance are carnal and unnecessary: what people who embrace this myth fail to understand is that carnality is only a choice, and can never be sponsored by wealth.

Whether in lack or in riches, people who decide to be carnal will still be carnal. This thought keeps them in a state of inertia and unproductiveness, building up in them an attitude of resentment towards wealth and successful people.

b. Thought of money (wealth) as the root of evil: This cliché, most common among religious people, is being misinterpreted and stems out from their attempts to make an excuse for their unproductiveness and for their resentment for successful people. Money has never been a root of evil but obsession for money to the extent that one can use any means whether good or bad to obtain it.

c. Thoughts of total irresponsibility but dependence on God alone for their wealth: these thought patterns have led to laziness, inactivity, indecision to those who embrace them. Such people would claim waiting for a miraculous day or incidence that will transit them from poverty to wealth without their work effort. As a Christian minister, I would like to be fair on this point to say that there may be a 50/50 chance for such miraculous occurrences:
- It may occur as God's reward to long term faithfulness of His people
- It may never occur, because it takes God and one's responsibility to build wealth and to be successful.

d. The thought that tithe is the only key to wealth: the concept of tithing as it pertains prosperity will be explained in subsequent chapters.

e. Thoughts that only few people are destined to be wealthy.
f. The thought that only a business idea assisted by capital is needed to grow into wealth. A business idea alone with capital is never the key to wealth. It takes more than that. In the introduction of this book, the story of Abel was told, he might have had a business idea and capital to start his business, but along the way, he arrived at a point of regret.

Note these Questions
- What if you were unable to manage and reinvest on already made profit?
- What if you added no creativity to your business?
- What if you had little regard for relationships in business?
- What if you are a baseline thinker and a poor risk taker?
- What if you had or borrowed a business idea but with poor habitual thoughts and bad character?
- What if you had poor financial literacy?
- What if you had bad communication qualities?

  Although wealthy thoughts not just an ordinary idea are the seeds of wealth, these thought must translate into many other qualities that are in resonance with each other (habits, administration, relationships, communication, action, courage, risk taking and financial literacy etc.)

g. Entitlement paradigm (thinking pattern, mentality): this is a thought pattern that assumes one's financial destiny to be the responsibility of someone else. Probably, spouse, family, godparents, government, friends, society. So many people who have held on to such thoughts, assuming entitled to assistance from men will always find themselves in disappointment. They blame circumstances, conditions, or conditioning for their behaviour. Their behaviour is not a product of their own conscious choice, based on values, but rather a product of their conditions, based on feeling
h. Thoughts of being unable to handle wealth and accept changes.
i. Wrong or misconceived thoughts of what formula for wealth and abundance is real.

Many, especially business individuals desire true wealth and are even taking steps in pursuit of that desire, however they may be victims of the wrong understanding of the wealth concept and formula and therefore pursuing it the wrong way.

THINK WEALTHY
The first step to financial freedom is to make the decision to be disciplined enough to adopt a changed thinking pattern. That pattern involves "thinking the wealthy way".

Financial freedom is not by chance, it is very predictable. Wealthy and successful people understand this fact and they thereby take proven steps that will lead them to abundance. One of the first steps they take

is the discipline of mental transition from the realm of poverty or the average to wealth. They ensure that they do the following:
   a. Think and decide to be wealthy: thoughts and decisions are one powerful combination in the subject of psycho-wealth. Decision is actually a strong desire for something backed up by the willingness to pay the price to obtain that thing. A thought emotionalized by strong desire will transit one to the realm of taking actions. Napoleon Hill also classified desire as the starting point to all achievement.
      Proof of decision for wealth
      - Accepting the responsibility for that decision
      - Taking action
      - Pursuing knowledge
      - Paradigm shift from reactivity (controlled by conditions) to proactiveness (act by choice)
      - Upgrading thoughts to wealthy thoughts
      - Upgrading to wealthy habits
      - Motivated by higher thoughts of other successful people.
   b. Search out, think and understand the mental transitions that bring wealth
      - They understand the law of attraction.
      - They understand the law of reality.
      - They fully understand the difference between and manifestations of the two mentalities of poverty and wealth, and try to adopt the wealthy one.

c. Think, know and apply the actual formula that will bring wealth.
d. They never wait (inertia state), but surround themselves with thoughts, people, situations, circumstances that are conducive to helping them realize the wealth they desire.

In the world of finances, there are two kinds of thinkers. These two thinkers use their mind's own creative power to channel their thoughts differently (persistently with regular and long term focus of those thoughts) towards an end. And since by the "law of attraction and reality", thoughts can be brought about in the material world by eventually altering our physical conditions.

1. *Higher thinkers*

These are people whose predominant thoughts are termed "higher thoughts". Higher thoughts although can be termed by wealthy people as wealthy thoughts, it could in other contexts refer to mean creative thoughts, positive thoughts, dream thoughts, idea thoughts, success thoughts, productive thoughts, pure thoughts and upgraded thoughts.

Higher thoughts go beyond just wealthy thoughts, they have to do with upgrading the brain to produce thoughts of high frequency vibrations to at least meet up the brain's potentials of creativity, prowess, will power, enlightenment, intelligence and "genius-ness". Higher thoughts will always consequently increase mental and physical productivity, income and wealth.

Characteristics of Higher thoughts
- High thought power
- High thought vibrations
  The concept of high thought power and vibrations will be explained in subsequent chapters.
- Characterized with burning desire
- Highly emotionalized
- Strong autosuggestion
- Result in organised planning and goal setting
- Accompanied with strong faith
- Enlightened thoughts (high learned thoughts)
- Definiteness of purpose
- Active and decisive
- Result in rich habit, rich attitude

2. **Baseline thinkers**:
   They are an opposite of thinkers who think high. These baseline thinkers have through their belief system, ideologies, indiscipline, non-upgraded mentality, conditioned their brain to think in a manner termed "baseline". On a broader view, it could mean; low, mediocre, average, and common, squander, unproductive, un-wealthy and poor thoughts. Consequently, this baseline thinking pattern will negatively affect their productivity, intelligence, income and money.

Characteristics of baseline thoughts
- State of inertia
- Lower thought vibrations
- Thoughts may be of lower or high energy (timeframe for transition into habits): a poor thought could translate quickly or slowly into a habit.

- Passive, reluctant
- Sometimes, indefiniteness of purpose
- Negative and poor autosuggestions
- Poorly emotionalized
- No burning desire
- Faithless
- Result in poverty habit; poverty attitude

LAW OF REALITY

This "law" has a very chilling parallel with the popular conservative law of attraction and states that:

"One's physical reality or condition (today) is a reflection of his/her thinking (yesterday)."

The physical condition or reality in this context would mean the absence or presence of physical financial fortune. "Thinking" also may be synonymic to "mindset". This law classifies people according to their physical (financial) reality as influenced by their mindset.

1. *Poor mindset – poor physical reality*: these kinds of people have a poor mindset (baseline thought, baseline thinking pattern) concerning success, wealth and life in general. Consequently, they live a life of poor physical reality of poverty and lack.

Cause

As said by Frederick Douglass, there is a cause to every effect. The effects of a poor mindset, which is a poor physical reality may be caused or influenced by the following;
- Entitlement mentality
- Dependency mentality

- reactive paradigm
- No investment (of the mind, talent or finances).
- Inherited thinking pattern (of baseline thoughts)
- Family experience and bad environmental influences
- Indiscipline, laziness
- Indebtedness
- Resentment for wealth and wealthy people
- Association with baseline thinkers
- Blamers

Effect:
- Poverty; insufficiency
- Desires change, but irresponsible and indecisive
- Hatred for wealthy people
- Only hopes
- No matter how much money and resource they are given, their mind-set and thoughts bring them back to zero.

2. *Wealthy (higher) mindset- poor physical reality*

This is a transition point between poor mindset-poor physical reality and higher mindset-wealthy physical reality.

Alteration or change of mindset is a decision and it happens faster in comparative to change of physical reality which takes awhile to be fully experienced. People at this stage still experience a poor physical reality, although they have adopted a better mindset and are taking necessary steps towards wealth. At this stage, persistence is what is required to reach the wealthy place. They are in between the place of poverty and the place of wealth. It is however sad that most people at this stage give up because of a yet un-experienced changed physical reality or just little progress.

Cause:
- Decision to change thought pattern
- Discipline to adopt a higher mindset
- Paradigm shifting
- Mind investment
- Investment in knowledge
- Investments rather than spending
- Self improvement
- Training
- Financial education

Effects:
- Little breakthrough
- On process
- Absence of physical cash
- Psychologically wealthy
- Proactive-ness
- Wealthy communications
- Persistence and continuous investment will certainly lead to wealth.

3. ***Wealthy (higher) mindset - wealthy physical reality:***

These kinds of people (higher thinkers) have arrived at the wealthy place after long term process of discipline and adopting a rich mindset, habits and lifestyle.

How do these people think and live?
- They are risk takers
- They believe in taking responsibility for the outcome of their lives.
- They engage in continuous investment of their minds.
- They do not allow criticism put down their thoughts and dreams.
- They possess positive mental attitude towards the opinion of others.
- They are patient people.
- They are careful over their financial resources.
- They believe in the law of process.
- They take action.
- They run, they do not rush.
- They see challenges as opportunities.

Effects:
- Abundance
- Physical cash
- Increased sphere of influence
- Respect and honour.

In the preceding pages of this book, a point was highlighted as one of the reason why wealthy people are indeed wealthy. That is "they think, know and apply the actual formula that brings wealth". Apart from the law of attraction and reality, there are formulas that determine and are responsible for the income of every working man. Applying these formulas strategically can increase the income index of any person. There are two formulas in the world of finances, one which is generic and the other specific to any profession or career that are responsible for your earning as a person or an organisation.

1. Formula of streams } ***Formula for wealth***
2. Formula of demand

FORMULA OF STREAMS
This is not actually particular to a profession or career but generally applies in incoming earnings. The formula simply defines that "the amount of money you receive as income will actually be in exact proportion to the number of income streams that flow to you".

Almost all very wealthy individuals never engage in only one stream of income or area of investment. Investment in a lone stream of income keeps you in the realm of "just enough" to meet immediate needs. More than one stream transits you to the realm of overflow or abundance.

Note
- The more your streams of income, the greater your income index
- Engage in streams of income that allow you express your talents and potentials.
- Multiple streams of income increase your sphere of influence
- When one stream fails, the others would compensate for it.

FORMULA OF DEMAND

No man as a liability can ever get paid an income. Every income that man earns was or is as a result of a service or product he rendered or provided. When demand for such services or product becomes limited or absent, the income index of the renderer runs down. The first key therefore to increasing your income is to realise that you are only paid for something being demanded for.

This formula of demand and of streams sum up to give what is known as the real formula for wealth and abundance.

Here is the formula of demand

"The amount of money you receive as income will be in exact proportion to:
1. The demand for your product and services.
2. Your ability (in providing/ rendering such product and services)
3. The scarcity of your kind."

THE DEMAND

Profit and loss, demand and supply are the dominant subjects in the world of economics. There is a fact that states; whenever there is supply of something demanded for, profit therefore would be made. In summary, any individual or organisation at any platform involved in providing services and products on high demand will always yield high income and grow wealthy. The cause of many financial and business frustrations is engaging in providing services or product of no or low demand. No more wonder, in our contemporary society, young people (undergraduates) are being forced by their parents to study some tagged "special" courses such as engineering, law or medicine. This is because demand for such professionals and their services are sufficient and sustainable as compared to practitioners of other fields of study.

Note:

- Never try to provide a service where there is no notable demand for it.
- Never invest in products not demanded for.
- Always respond to demand and your income will increase.
- The cause of poverty is lack of response to any demand.
- The higher your demand index, the higher your income

In entrepreneurship, when working on providing a service, demand could be;
- Created
- Satisfied, if already existing

"THOUGHT AND DEMAND CREATION"
Creating a demand entails establishing the desire for your products in people's heart. Creating a demand may require the use of the creative faculty of the brain. This faculty provides thought creation stimuli when in use, creating thoughts of how to make and satisfy the demand for a service.

Businesses and sales organisations employ and pay their marketers and sales persons for effort and time invested in putting the brain and thoughts to work on how to increase the demand index for the services rendered by such organisation.

Your thoughts, words and actions must:
- Motivate buyers to buy your products
- Influence the emotions of a prospective buyer
- Convince customers that some particular needs of theirs will be fulfilled by your product or service better than by other products available in the market
- Increase buying desire
- Reduce in the heart of prospective customers, the fear of loss
- Express the values and benefit that a prospective buyer will receive if he buys what you are selling
- Demonstrate the basic and secondary needs that your product can satisfy.

SATISFYING EXISTING DEMANDS OR NEEDS
Every man has certain basic human needs whether short term or long term. These needs motivate him to give out money for their satisfaction. Identifying some of these important needs of people and satisfying them increase your wealth index.

a. Daily needs: these are basic needs or products that are on demand every day – water (bottled water, drinks), soap (especially bathing soap), food (restaurant, snacks).
b. Money: this is an important need of man. Every man wants more money to himself, therefore providing services or products that can make or save money for people increases your income.
c. Security
d. Health (hospital, supplements, fitness)
e. Spiritual (counselling, prayers)

    f. Communication (internet, social media, mobile phone, blogging)
    g. Education (schools, public speaking, writing)

YOUR ABILITY *(in providing/rendering product/service)*

Ability is the skill employed in the application of creative imagination and thoughts. Ability should entail skills, prowess, proficiency, competence, excellence, mastery, eloquence or exceptionality. It enables one to become a pacesetter in what he or she does.

When you are ABLE to provide services or product in a manner better than others, your income index shall increase.

YOUR ABILITY AND THE BRAIN: Ability (skill) is one of the qualities of the brain power. It comes from repeated actions and use of a permanent neural pathway until a habitual process becomes so easy, faster and efficient to do (even in sub consciousness). Your ability can appreciate by engaging your brain and mind in long term learning, training, and practice. Every individual starts off in any endeavour with limited knowledge and knows how that could benefit them and others. As they practice and learn more, their ability increases and they become more valuable. With more value, come more earnings.

NOTE

- The world (marketplace) yearns for competence.
- Developing skills and competence requires discipline and persistence
- Psychological, physical and intellectual knowhow is required to satisfy demand and motivate people to return to you.
- More than sixty percent of humanity adds no skill to what they do.
- Upgrade your brain, upgrade your competence.
- Higher thinkers are skilful people.

SCARCITY OF YOUR KIND

When you increase so much your ability and become extremely competent, your kind becomes scarce. The scarcity of your kind defines how irreplaceable you can be in your field of endeavour. When you are in "a class of your own", a pacesetter, leader, a resource in your field or business, men will search out for you and pay you for who you are and what you have.

NOTE

- Become scarce by renovating and investing mentally.
- Become scarce by upgrading your brain.
- Become scarce by mastery.
- Character adds or removes from your ability
- Follow the leaders and become a leader.
- Invest much time in self-improvement.
- Be committed to lifelong learning.

Professionalism on a professional level is also an indicator of competence; it connotes excellence in standard of practice and conduct. What improves your professionalism includes;
- Your ability to be beneficent
- Your ability to be non- maleficent
- Justice (equality in service provision)

Financial freedom in individual lives, homes, organisations, communities is very much required to drive the "right revolutions" needed to better our world, but this freedom unknown to many begins from the brain. Every quality that is a requirement or consequence of professionalism, skills, ability, competence, creating and satisfying demand were built up habits originating from "thoughts".

Financial freedom therefore from the brain begins with:
- A mental shift
- Adopting a wealthier thinking pattern
- Thinking "high"

A MENTAL SHIFT: a conclusion of what has been said is that, for financial freedom to begin, first, a mental shift from poverty, lack, average or survival consciousness to wealth, abundance and prosperity consciousness must occur. The mind has to be cleared from its wrong concepts about finances and adopt the right concepts, before it starts to manifest.

ADOPTING A WEALTHIER THINKING PATTERN: There is a way "rich people think." Such ways and pattern must be studied and adopted. They invest on thoughts that vibrate at a rate that will attract to them their physical counterpart of wealth. Wealthy people look upon the world around them and see opportunities to succeed or make money from it rather than just surviving in it.

THINKING HIGH: the ability to think high stems from possessing a healthy thinking pattern and lifestyle. Thinking high requires the use of the creative potentials of the brain in boosting your general success-index. Higher thoughts are thoughts of high energy and vibrations which are yielded EASILY by brains receptive to such thoughts.

How the brain becomes more receptive to creative and higher thoughts is what the process of brain upgrade should address!

CHAPTER FOUR: HIGHER THOUGHTS

Just as in physics, "every reaction is a result of an opposite action". The bodily system operates in like manners; every response generated comes from a stimulus created. Thoughts in the thought creation centre of the brain are generated when what I call thought creation stimulus travels to the creation centre to cause thought vibrations. These thought vibrations would continue to a particular level or pitch sufficient enough to form thoughts. Higher thoughts are thoughts of very high vibrations and thought power.

Understanding some of these thought-terms as thought power and vibrations are essential if we must fully grasp the process of brain upgrade.

THOUGHT POWER: defines the amount of energy of thought vibrations in transit (from creation point to storage point or habitual transition point).

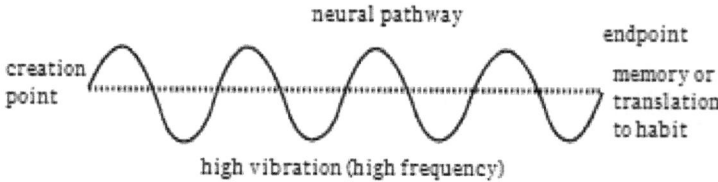
high vibration (high frequency)

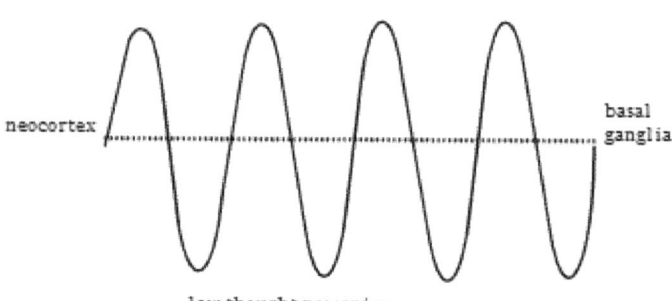
low thought power/ energy

Thought vibrations of high energy are able to translate into habits much more quickly as compared to thoughts vibrations of lower energy. Most times, thoughts of high vibrations result in highly energized thoughts, while those of low vibrations produce thoughts energy of accompanying proportion.

Persistently engaging the brain over "a particular thought" increases the energy of that thought.

In conclusion, the energy of a thought determines how fast such a thought becomes habits.

THOUGHT VIBRATIONS

The human brain receives thoughts in vibrations caused by thought creation stimuli. These thought creation stimuli could be internal or external. The external thought creation stimuli are sourced from the outside world and they interact or communicate with our mind by the means of our five senses:

- Sight
- Sound
- Smell
- Sensation/feeling
- Taste

Through the medium of external thought stimuli, every human brain is capable of picking up "thought vibrations" of thought released by other people's brain (thinking). For example, by this medium:

- We pick up thoughts from reading through sight other people's thoughts (writings).

- We pick up creative imaginations and thoughts by the sight of other people's creative work and thoughts (paintings, innovations).
- We pick up thoughts by listening through the ears the words of other people.
- We pick up thoughts (of maybe what we choose to eat) by the work of the taste stimuli.

Internal thought creation stimuli on the other hand come from within and may be sourced from experience (memory), imagination (imaginative faculty), autosuggestion, and the subconscious mind.

When the brain is stimulated by these various thought creation stimuli, it vibrates at low frequency. When the vibrations continue or are stepped up to a considerable or nominal rate, it becomes properly what is known as thought. Thought then travel to where it is stored for long-term or short-term usage or translated into habits, words or behaviour etc.

The vibrations of thought are influenced also by emotions and motivations. Through such influences, the vibrations of thought may be increased or stepped up. The brain when stimulated by emotions and motivations vibrates at a much more rapid rate then it does without emotions and motivations. The role of these emotions and motivations is to help increase the rate of thought vibrations above the ordinary even to such a pitch that the brain becomes highly receptive to the thoughts (or ideas) coming from the thought creation stimuli (internal or external).

These emotions and motivations could be positive or

negative. Both positive and negative emotions and motivations cannot at the same time occupy or stimulate the brain. One or the other must dominate. These emotions/motivations have sources, and so, in order to cultivate the habit of applying and using positive emotions and motivations, you must find the source and allow it to fully influence you.

Negative emotions/motivation should be avoided because although they also increase thought vibrations, they surely negate or destroy one's chances of prosperity and happiness.

There are various types of positive and negative emotions/motivations which basically include:

Positive emotions/ motivations

- emotions/motivations of enthusiasm
- emotions/motivations of sex (in marriage only)
- emotions/motivations of hope/promise
- emotions/motivations of right words/praise
- emotions/motivations of love
- emotions/motivations of strong desire
- emotions/motivations of recognition
- emotions/motivations of faith

Negative emotions/motivations

- emotions/motivations of fear
- emotions/motivations of alcoholism/ drugs
- emotions/motivations of detrimental habits; smoking, gambling etc.
- emotions/motivations of jealousy/envy

- emotions/ motivations of regret
- emotions/ motivations of revenge/ anger
- emotions/motivations of criticism/wrong words
- emotions/ motivations of greed
- emotions/ motivations of hatred

EXTERNAL THOUGHT CREATION STIMULI

The outside world can influence our thought by communicating with the brain through the five senses. The result of the five sense interaction stimulates the brain to vibrate until thoughts are formed.

Sight:

People think by what they see. The brain picks up images and actions (dynamic or static) as stimuli from the outside world and vibrates until thoughts about what is sighted are created or modified. The images of the outside world are products of the thoughts of other people (men or God) and can be classified into

a. sight of nature (God's creations; God's thoughts, highest thinker)
b. Sight of man's creation (man's innovations, writings, painting, inventions; man's thoughts).

Sound:

People think by the words they hear. Words are products of thoughts, which means people can think the thought of others by listening to their words. Thoughts are transformed into words in the broca's area (portion) of the left frontal lobe. These words when heard become stimulus that vibrate the brain of the hearer until they become thoughts. The different types of speakers or words that influence thoughts could include;

- a. Man's own words
- Speaking to himself of an already known fact
- Word of self suggestion and opinion
- Inner voice (conscience or intuition)

- b. Words of others
- Media
- Preachers
- Critics
- Friends and family
- Teachers, colleagues, and from the general public.
- c. Supernatural voices

Feeling and sensations

Many times also, thoughts are created (about people and their circumstances) or they change according to one's physical contact with them and also by their expressed facial and bodily gestures.

When two people have physical contact and touch, stimuli travel to their brain to vibrate them, creating thoughts (perceptions) about each other. These created thoughts then prompt an individual to react (whether favourable or not) in response to that thoughts and his perceptions. Examples of such contact may include;

- Hand shaking and holding
- Hugs and romance
- Sexual contact
- Physical conflict/abuse

These contacts could create thoughts of whether;

- Being loved, resented, liked or hated
- Being honoured and dishonoured
- Being welcomed or rejected, neglected.

Positive contacts create excitements, motivation, agreement, love, resolutions etc.

Negative contacts create lustful thoughts, unreasonable arousal, conflicts etc.

INTERNAL THOUGHT CREATION STIMULI

Thoughts/thoughts vibrations can be created by thought creation stimuli formed inside the brain/mind itself. The stimuli when excited travel from their source point to the thought creation site to cause vibration up to the required rate or pitch that can bring about thought. These internal stimuli could be sourced from;

- Memory
- Subconscious mind
- Autosuggestion
- Imagination

MEMORY: Both the limbic system and neocortex of the brain take part in memory storage (long term and short term). Thought creation stimuli could come from already stored experience and information in the memory. These stimuli then travel to cause thought vibrations that modify, recall, change, transform, revise, refashion, remodel, or apply the stored memory-information. These thoughts may even cause behavioural changes according to the experience with people and events in one's life.

The content of a person's memory could stem from these two major sources;

    a. Experiences; such as relationships with people, family and environmental influences, life occurrences, events, incidence or encounters.
    b. Information: Knowledge is directly proportional to information acquired. Information itself is acquired through the learning process (education). Education could be formal and informal. Information is acquired from; books, media, parental teaching, religious information, culture, discoveries or researches

SUBCONSCIOUS MIND

The subject of the mind itself is very complex and in order to fully understand how the subconscious mind could be a source of thought creation stimuli, it is important to know how the subconscious mind works. The mind is separated into both the conscious and the subconscious. According to Sigmund Freud, founder of psychoanalysis, the human mind could be compared to an iceberg.

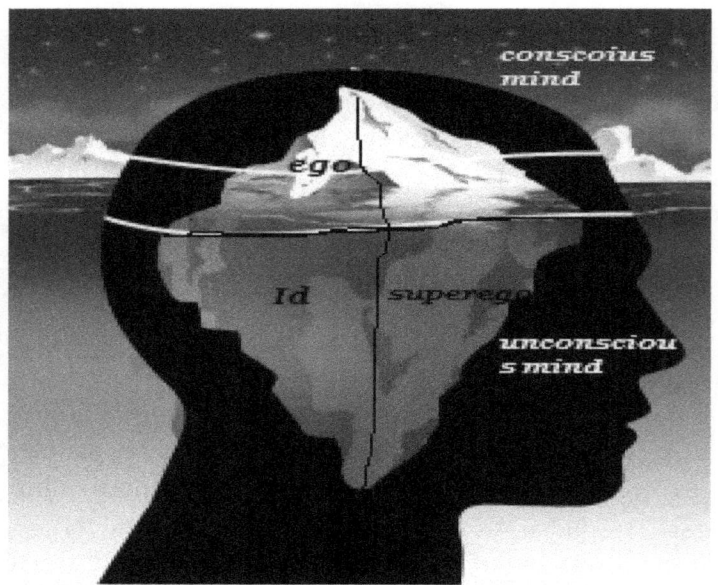

He suggested that the part of the iceberg above the water represents consciousness and the vast region below the surface represents the subconscious mind. He went on to say that there are three basic personality structures that make up the mind; Id, Ego and Superego. As even illustrated in the above diagram, of all three, only the Id is totally unconscious. The function of the subconscious mind is to store and retrieve data. It can be compared to a huge memory bank where its capacity is virtually unlimited. It actually stores permanently all events, thoughts, circumstances, actions, habits that have ever occurred.
According to Napoleon Hill in his book "Think and Grow Rich", the subconscious mind is a field of consciousness in which every impulse of thought that reaches the objective mind through any of the five

senses is classified and recorded and from which thoughts may be recalled or withdrawn as letters may be taken from a filling cabinet"

The subconscious mind works as a cycle. Every data contained therein once occurred in the conscious mind but later found its way to the subconscious mind with or without the knowledge of the mind bearer. Brian Tracy compared the subconscious mind to a garden or fertile soil in which seeds germinate and grow while the conscious mind as the gardener planting the seeds.

The subconscious mind is a storehouse for infinite intelligence. Research has shown that at the age of 21 years, one would have stored more than a hundred times the contents of the entire encyclopaedia Britannica. Under hypnosis, people could recall events from thirty years before with perfect clarity. The subconscious mind therefore becomes the link between the finite mind or brain and infinite intelligence. In the creation of thoughts, stimuli from the field of infinite intelligence could travel to the place of thought creation, vibrating it to produce thoughts.

The subconscious mind functions voluntarily whether effort is made or not to influence it. They suggested to people thoughts that can expresses itself in one's physical reality.

AUTOSUGGESSTION

This means self suggestion. This occurs when a thought becomes or acts as stimuli for the creation of other thoughts.

The subconscious mind is also fed by the principle of autosuggestion. It is the link of interaction between the conscious part of the mind where conscious thoughts take place and the base of action for the subconscious mind.

IMAGINATION

The imagination process is believed to be the right brain function and a mental process of the conscious mind. Imagination creates in the conscious mind something new in form of images, ideas, initiatives, concepts or processes never experienced or perceived before.

The ability to imagine is one of the most powerful abilities of the human brain and a strong force that has enabled man to almost change the course of nature. Modernization, civilization, industrialization, science, technology, discoveries and researches are all products of the creative process of human imagination.

Many scholars have tried providing an extensive list of kinds of imagination that could occur in the mind of man to include but not limited to; effectuations, fantasy, constructions, strategy, empathy, reconstruction, passive and emotional imaginations, but conclusively all these imaginations depend on whether they are creative or synthetic as classified by the writer "Napoleon Hill".

SYNTHETIC IMAGINATION (reasoning faculty): This imagination is not originally creative but works upon already existing idea, initiative, plans, and knowledge to create a new, re-arranged or improved form of them.

CREATIVE IMAGINATION (creative faculty): These imaginations initiate new ideas and processes in the mind. Creative imaginations are usually made active by strong desire and constant usage.

When imaginations are initiated, thought creation stimuli from the imaginative faculty travel at high speed to the place of thought creation. These stimuli are very strong and can cause thought vibrations of exceedingly rapid rate. When the vibrations produce thoughts, they still continue to vibrate rapidly until "higher thoughts" are produced.

Thoughts when created enable the analysis, breakdown, understanding, interpretation and expression of what was imagined.

All thoughts and hunches that are formed in the brain are generated from these sources whether internal or external. Man from these thought sources have generated all the thoughts that come to and from the brain. Through his thoughts, man has discovered and harnessed more of nature's forces through time. Man has overcome gravity that he can fly faster than the fastest birds in the air. He has harnessed the atmosphere and made it serve as a means of instantaneous communication with any part of the world. Man has through these thoughts analyzed and determined the consisting elements of the sun and even its distances from the earth. He has created objects of artificial intelligence and technology that can make life easy for him. He has increased the speed of locomotion, and can get to a place more than three hundred miles away in just an hour. Man has created, and surfed thoroughly the web until he can see any point on the earth, and make money just sitting in his room.

Man's only limitation, lies in the upgrade and use of his brain. He is yet to reach the greatest height of his thinking. He only has found out that he can think, and he is using it the nominal way. If he must think high, he must upgrade the brain.

CHAPTER FIVE: BRAIN UPGRADE

Dr. Jeffrey Fannin, founder of the centre for cognitive enhancement once said "all thoughts are nothing more than energy and information".
Higher thoughts possess more power (higher energy) which means, as compared to thoughts of lower energy, it could create a neural pathway connected to the basal ganglia and repeating these thoughts would however in much lesser time translate into habits. Higher thoughts are also of higher thought vibrations, more rapid than ordinary thoughts. It is possible to condition and train the brain to a point whereby it becomes highly receptive to higher thoughts, reasoning beyond the communal way.
On a broader scale, traversing even into the Christian views of what this higher thought could mean; higher thoughts are actually seeds of greatness, yet the result of using the creative power of the brain and mind. All great men in history were higher thinkers because they were able to think the uncommon way thereby doing uncommon things. God himself, the creator, is a higher thinker, and in fact the highest thinker. Every work of creation (the universe, the galaxies, the comets, the planets, supernatural beings, man...) originated first from the thoughts of his mind.
Isaiah 55:8-9
"for my thoughts are not your thought, neither are your ways my ways saith the lord. For as the heavens are higher than the earth, so are my ways higher than your way, and my thoughts than your thoughts"
God, the highest thinker in the universe created man, his physical form and immaterial spirit. No wonder the

brain is remarkable, well designed and surpasses anything that man has created. And if we believe that we are created in the image of God, which means our ability to think is one aspect of our having been made in the image of God. We are reminded in Isaiah 55:9 that God is the highest thinker and that his thoughts are above our thoughts. We can never reach God's level of thinking, however by his leave, he expects Man to think and live up to the potentials he has placed in him. God expects us to think as high as possible expressing creativity; extending creation and profiting humanity.

Every individual that has profited humanity in history came to a point whereby they recognized there was a problem to solve. Moving ahead to solve these problems requires the initial step of thinking high and then taking actions. In other words, higher thoughts are the foundation for everything created or problem solved on the earth and in the universe.

In order to have a broader understanding of what higher thought could mean in any context (especially in a Christian concept), here are 100 facts about higher thoughts.

HUNDERED FACTS ABOUT HIGHER THOUGHTS (Christian perspective)

1. Higher thoughts are the power of creativity.
2. Success is determined by the power of creativity (higher thinking).
3. Dreams are fruits of higher thoughts.
4. Ideas, innovations and inventions are products of higher thoughts.
5. Man's creations come from his ability to think.
6. Everything we see in the world is thought MATERALIZED.

7. They are wealthy thoughts, dream thoughts or idea thoughts.
8. They are divinely planted ideas.
9. Thoughts of aspirations and achievements.
10. They are carriages of success
11. Higher thoughts can be put into action, or ignored. It is a choice.
12. Higher thoughts, put into action, habitualized, must pass through process (time) to become productive (fruitful).
13. At the initial stage, people (many times, majority) may not believe or agree with ones higher thought.
14. Criticism can be a de-motivator to higher thinking.
15. A higher thinker must persist to the end.
16. Every human brain has the potentials in it to think high.
17. They are explored and or yet unexplored abilities of the mind.
18. The quality of a man's life is the makeup of his thoughts.
19. Inability to recognize problems can hinder higher thinking.
20. Higher thought can be stolen, if shared prematurely in the wrong associations.
21. Information is a booster to higher thinking.
22. Strong desire for a particular higher thought causes one to pursue it.
23. Higher thinkers nurture and protect their thoughts.
24. The opposite of higher thoughts are baseline thoughts.

25. Pure thoughts are also higher thoughts, they brighten the mind.
26. Impure thoughts darken the mind.
27. The higher, the bigger and wealthier a thought is, the longer it takes to process into physical reality.
28. There are four stages in a thought-goal chain
    - Conception of thought
    - Action stage
    - Process
    - Reaching goal
29. We grow by our ability to think high.
30. The highest form of thought is the "God-thought".
31. Higher thoughts are the heart desires of a soul.
32. Great personalities are higher thinkers.
33. All previously tagged impossible achievements once coincided as thought in people's brain.
34. Write down your higher thoughts or lose it.
35. Discouragement and disappointment are higher thoughts de-motivators.
36. Every man can think.
37. Higher thought inspires the pursuit of destiny.
38. Higher thoughts without positive desire and action become mere daydreaming.
39. Higher thinkers rule the world.
40. Higher thoughts increase one's potentials.
41. Higher thoughts bring priority to one's life.
42. Higher thinkers are hopeful people.
43. Greater thinkers balance creativity with character.
44. High thinkers follow higher thinkers.
45. Great thinkers follow godly counsel.

Higher Thoughts

46. Higher thoughts in a dark mind can contaminate our world.
47. Great thinkers are God followers.
48. God wants us to think "VERY BIG".
49. You can do anything if you think and believe it.
50. Start acting NOW, if you want your thoughts to produce.
51. The mother of multiple thoughts is a thought.
52. Invest in your thoughts.
53. You must learn to deal with the 3fs in the pursuit of your higher thoughts:
    - Fear
    - Frustration
    - Failure
54. Great revolutions began in the brain of men.
55. The comfort zone is the enemy of "higher thought" pursuit.
56. Higher thinkers are patient.
57. Divine thinkers always encounter divine opportunity.
58. A higher thinker who encounters JESUS has the power to change the world.
59. God Himself is a thinker.
60. If you follow God, then he will give you divine thoughts.
61. Bad character demotes higher thoughts.
62. A careless thinker can lose his dreams.
63. Thoughts can be upgraded.
64. Your close associates affect your ability to think high.
65. If you desire uncommon success and achievement, you then must think uncommon higher thoughts.

66. Only less than 10% of humanity thinks 'higher thoughts'.
67. More than 50% of humanity thinks they are thinking, but actually they are only worrying.
68. Your thoughts affect your words.
69. Talkative people think the less.
70. Thinkers must be learners.
71. Always keep the "thought" clean.
72. Sin renders a higher thinker useless.
73. The words of the bible boost the brain the most.
74. Let your strongest emotions drive you to pursue higher thinking, not the opposite sex.
75. The weaker your mind, the weaker your thoughts.
76. Man is greater than the other, if he can think better.
77. There should be a connection between one's higher thought and divine purpose.
78. You must allow God to use your thoughts, if you want it to be meaningful to humanity.
79. Fight for your THOUGHTS.
80. You must deal with spiritual head attackers and thought killers by the weapon of prayer.
81. Thoughts can also be influenced spiritually.
82. Great thinkers are never time wasters.
83. You must pray about your thoughts, dream, goal and aspirations every day.
84. The world will always honour great thinkers.
85. Higher thinkers seek out mentors and coaches.
86. Goals are higher thoughts with a target.
87. Never share higher thought with people of no thought, they will waste it.

88. Do not be in inertia, but be willing to modify your thought when necessary.
89. Your thought without God is foolishness.
90. Higher thoughts add value to your life.
91. Higher thinkers are the most creatively imaginative.
92. Thinking is beyond intellectualism.
93. The word genius is referred to people who think "HIGH".
94. You must be constructively discontented with your present state to pursue your "higher thoughts".
95. Run, but do not rush your thoughts.
96. Negative habits can neutralize positive thoughts.
97. Thinkers respect, communicate and associate with other greater thinkers.
98. Man is brightened by his higher thoughts.
99. Keep your brain and thoughts alive and boosted by feeding them.
100. The beginning of all achievement is "thoughts".

Brain upgrade increases the receptiveness of the brain to "high" thoughts. Overall, it improves total brain productivity. The onetime television show "limitless" which explores the fiction of unlocking the full potentials of the human brain through meditation. In a story on the show, a so called pill supposedly allows the brain to work at superhuman efficiency, giving the user perfect recall and leaps of intuitive insight. In reality however, there is no such pills, but there are proven ways to improve total brain efficiency and thinking pattern.

Brain upgrade addresses the underlying reasons of problems as poor personal growth, low productivity, poor mindset, low IQ etc. It concerns the growth and betterment of the mind/brain including improvement of memory, perception, logical reasoning, problem solving skill, intelligence and hypothetical thinking. It cuts across improving skills and competence, effective communication abilities (speaking, writing), coordination, wealth creation, processing capacity, brain strength and body function.

Recent researches and findings in neuroscience strongly affirm the possibilities of using certain approaches aimed at enhancing brain performance. Neuroplasticity is proven to exist which is the ability to reshape the nervous system and brain, and studies have shown repeatedly that with certain training and supplements, cognitive enhancement and improved intelligence can be attained.

However, this book shall itself highlight approaches that are biblically based and affirmed to upgrade the brain.

As Christians, we believe that the "word of God" is our sure word of prophesy. This word of God affirms to us in Genesis 1:26-27 that God created all of humanity (man) in the image of Himself (Isaiah 1:18) and our physical form with a well designed brain should have the ability to reason and operate in the best of ways.

Our major problem came however when Adam according to Genesis 3:1-19 rebelled against his Creator and the lord cursed the earth. This curse has resulted in the many woes of mankind (disease, suffering and ultimately death). The human brain and the mind did not escape the effects of the curse. Our inability and unwillingness to reason and think the best way; "the higher way" is caused, either directly or indirectly by the effects of the fall.

God, in his absolute clemency, takes step to restore many aspects of mankind. For example, he provided animal skin to cover man's nakedness; he gave rain needed to bring up crops from the earth. And he also provided herbs (as plants) to cure any of man's diseases. God also knows and recognizes that the brain of man dictates the boundaries of his intellectual capacity and that how man thinks and perceives the world impacts his ability to rise to any challenges. God knows that the ability to imagine in man is what he needs to achieve anything on earth. In this wise, God by his word provided approaches on how to grow up to express the full potentials of the brain he has given him. Surprisingly, yet interestingly, these biblical strategies have very chilling parallels and correlate very closely to several scientific approaches to this purpose (brain upgrade).

Brain upgrade and Intelligence

Intelligence is not fixed. Studies have shown it can be increased. Upgrading the brain would definitely improve IQ and ability to reason abstractly. Irrespective of environmental interactions, genetic influences, sex, race, or region, working out the brain with these approaches will certainly step up your IQ above present level.

Brain Upgrade and Wealth Creation

The human brain and mind were created to possess and express a rich mindset (belief system) that is alien to poverty. The brain is like the hardware of a computer. A computer has a memory capacity and a central processor that can access memory and process it. But a computer (that is the brain) won't work properly unless it also has the right software (mindset). The computer's programming must be consistent with its design and free of viruses that can slow its performances. The process of brain upgrade frees the mind from viruses (poverty and negative mindsets) and exposes us to information that changes our belief systems and in turn alters our priorities and way of life. Note that according to the law of reality, your wealthy mindset will always culminate into wealthy physical reality after undergoing the proper processing.

Brain Upgrade and Higher Thoughts

Upgrading the brain increases its receptiveness to higher thoughts and enables us have a better understanding of any thought being transmitted from a thought creation stimuli

Brain Upgrade and the Highest Thinker

"God is the highest thinker". It is written in his word (3 John1:2) that our soul (mind) should prosper. Brain upgrade does not exclude the spiritual belief system of the mind.

God designs our mind to operate within biblical worldview and he desires that we fill up our minds with His thoughts documented in his words (the scripture). He calls it the Truth. God challenges the sinful man to repent of his ways and his thoughts (Isaiah 55:7-9). Reasons are that the sinful man does not think like God and their ways are not God's ways. The sinner's way displaces the Lord and destroys the individual. God expects us to base our thinking and our ways upon God's thoughts and God's ways as revealed in His word (Matthew 7: 24-25).

If we must base our approaches to brain upgrade on the scripture, then it becomes indispensably necessary to submit our thinking pattern to God. Brain upgrade therefore works on our spirituality to bring us to the point of submission to God's word.

Brain upgrade and Motivation

The motivational system of the brain monitors the state of satisfaction of any goals we have set and activates behaviours to meet any need that arises.

Brain upgrade works on the motivational mechanism in the brain and brightens our state of being. It also induces structural changes inside the brain that cause same behaviour with the record of leading to greater productivity to be repeated always.

HOW TO UPGRADE THE BRAIN BIBLICALLY
1. READING

2 timothy 2:15 *KJV "Study to show thyself approved unto God, a workman that needeth not to be ashamed, rightly dividing the word of truth."*

Proverb 1:5 ESV *"Let the wise hear and increase in learning, and the one who understands obtain guidance"*

Scriptures admonish its readers by these verses to study and learn more and more. Reading is the primary way we can study, learn and educate ourselves, and a basic way of upgrading the brain. With only a few exceptions, we can go as far as to say that if reading is alien to a person, then his or her brain is dying.

Jesus, during his earthly ministry always seemed surprised at the lack of understanding of the Pharisees and scribes to what they claim to know and he challenges them by asking *"...have you not read?"*

The act of reading is the tool that has brought civilization and modernization to humanity and society. It has brought enlightenment to man's mind and made man better. Reading has traditionally been and still is one of the main ways we acquire formal knowledge, become informed and get smarter.

Written words, inscriptions, or paintings that are written, printed, inscribed or painted in books or other readable materials translate into thought creation stimuli when engaged on in the process of reading.

Two senses that interact with the external environment are activated during reading; the eyes and the ears. They capture these written words and as thought creation stimuli, they travel to the thought creation centre of the brain causing thought vibrations and eventually thoughts. Those eventual thoughts created concern the subject matter of interest contained in the book. These thoughts may add understanding, increase inquisition, and prompt more readings about and around the subject matter of interest. In other ways, reading also adds or stores into the limitless capacity of infinite intelligence in the subconscious mind. It activates man's creative imagination and increases the volume of knowledge (and experience) stored in the memory.

Words written in books are the documentations of other thinkers and the reading process is the way in which thoughts are shared among people and thinkers. In order to upgrade your brain therefore, books written by thinkers of thoughts, higher than yourself or your level of knowledge concerning any subject must be read. Reading books of higher thinkers than yourself makes you tap into the wealth of their minds and associate with their thinking pattern.

In such case, where written words of higher thinkers are read, the brain does not really work at producing such higher thoughts on its own, but higher thoughts of these higher thinkers are provided already, for the brain to process or modify and store at an appropriate site.

When you want to upgrade your brain and you begin to read frequently (or every day), higher thoughts or written words of higher thinkers in a particular field, the brain automatically after a period of workout, becomes very receptive to higher thoughts. The brain at this point can now produce higher thoughts of its own from the bulk of experience and knowledge it has acquired. The retentive abilities of the brain is increased and because the brain now operates at a higher level than it was before, it could now with all ease and even in sub consciousness recall thoughts or knowledge from the level it was operating formally. Upgrade your brain more, by moving ahead to read higher thoughts of other higher thinkers.

By engaging in long-term reading, especially for younger brains, the imaginative faculty of man becomes more developed, and creative imagination becomes more alert in proportion to its development also through use.

In the world of finances, reading is the act that brings knowledge. However, knowledge is only potential power and will never become power if such knowledge is not organised into definite and practical plans of action and directed to a definite end (of yielding money). Knowledge (information) could be generalized which plays a little role in the making of financial freedom or yielding of money. Knowledge could also be specialized.

Specialized knowledge is required before you can be sure of your ability to translate your thoughts and desires into a wealthy physical reality. This specialized knowledge is of services, professions, businesses, products intended to be offered in return for money. Knowledge may have no value except it is gained by its application towards a productive returning end.

Successful people never stop acquiring specialized knowledge related to their major callings, while those who make the mistake of assuming learning ends in the classroom usually end up unsuccessful. As Napoleon Hill would say, *"Schooling does but little more than to put one in the way of learning how to acquire practical knowledge."* The man of God, David Oyedepo would say also, "Schooling only makes you literate, it is investment in literature that creates your actual future." The way of success is the way of continuous pursuit of knowledge and he who stops studying merely because he has finished school is on his way to mediocrity, whatever be his calling.

After the desire and the decision to acquire specialized knowledge, you must decide of what sort, the purpose for which it is needed, the goal toward which you are working and your major life's purpose. This will also help in the sourcing of relevant specialized knowledge; it may be sourced from;

a. University and other forms and levels of higher education
b. Special training courses
c. Libraries
d. Association or cooperation with other higher thinkers or specialists. It is called by many, the master mind alliance.
e. Independent studies and researches

However, for reading generally and also for upgrading the brain and becoming smarter, here are five suggested categories of books that will help make sure you are getting a well-rounded reading experience preparing you for the society today and tomorrow. But, if all of your reading falls outside of these five categories, you then are probably reading more for entertainment than for upgrading your brain:

a. Books related to the area of your present calling.
b. Books related to the expertise or endeavour you will need to be competitive in 5 years.
c. Books on topic from a completely different field.
d. Classical literature
e. The bible (written words of the highest thinker)

2. **THINKING**

Joshua 1:8 *" This Book of the Law shall not depart from your mouth, but you shall MEDITATE on it day and night, so that you may be careful to do according to all that is written in it. For then you will make your way prosperous, and then you will have good success."*

1 Corinthians 14:20 ESV *"Brothers, do not be children in your THINKING. Be infants in evil, but in your thinking be mature."*

2 Timothy 2:7 ESV *"THINK over what I say, for the Lord will give you understanding in everything."*

Philippians 4:8 ESV *"Finally, brothers, whatever is true, whatever is honourable, whatever is just, whatever is pure, whatever is lovely, whatever is commendable, if there is any excellence, if there is anything worthy of praise, THINK about these things."*

In the first scripture enlisted above, Joshua 1:8, God, the highest thinker commands and endorses the act of meditation. Meditation means musing about a particular matter of interest (of which in this case, God specifies that such musing should be about "his thoughts" as written in His words). Meditation is a religious interpretation of what thinking is. Therefore it can be said of that, God commands us to think, for by that, it would translate into "doing" (habits) then eventually making our way prosperous (successful physical reality).

In the next scripture (1corinthians 4:20), Peter the servant of God, admonishes us to be mature, not children in thinking.

How does a child think?
- Foolishly - baseline - unprofitable - uncreative - fantastical

Mature thinking would mean on the other hand, higher thoughts, creative and profitable. This writer of two epistles of the New Testament expects and encourages his reader and by extension the church and all of humanity to engage in higher thinking as an intentional and structured act and not just in casual circumstances.

In the words of Paul in 2 Timothy 2:7, Paul commands Timothy to "think" over what he had said to him. However, here is an interesting question. Why should Timothy and by extension, we as believers "think" when already he Timothy and we ourselves have heard what

Paul had to say? It is because of the same effect Paul himself had highlighted in the same verse; it is by the act and process of thinking that we could critically analyse and gain proper understanding of the words we hear or read.

Lastly, Philippians 4:8 gives us elements or qualities of thoughts that should characterize our thinking pattern or thought life. In previous chapters, I made mention that the Christian or biblical views of higher thoughts are right and pure thoughts. Also, they are thoughts that are considered excellent, commendable and praise worthy, not foolish, baseline, uncreative and unproductive thoughts. We can conclusively go as far as to say that this verse commands us to think "high".

Thinking (meditation) is an act which when done deliberately, upgrades the brain. We think all the time, but most of us do not spend any structures, intentional time just thinking. We think just enough to begin our next action. There is a fact that more than 90% of humanity do not take deliberate time to think productively at all. It is by taking time to deliberately sit and think that we upgrade our brain and think "high". Higher thoughts do not just come by casual thinking but by process of deliberate thinking. One reason why most people do not take time to sit and deliberately think is that it usually just becomes day dreaming. Day dreaming isn't necessarily a bad thing, but it isn't as directed as what you will be trying to achieve by sitting and thinking.

The act of deliberate thinking directed towards achieving a goal activates the creative imagination of the mind. It alerts almost all the senses that interact with the outside world and the sources of internal thought stimuli to get to work, sourcing out thought creation stimuli that could create thought vibration of higher frequency which eventually becomes higher thought

In taking steps to upgrade your brain by deliberate thinking, you must find sources of higher thoughts from the outside world through interactions or exposure to higher thinkers and their activities or through the persistent use of the imaginative faculty of the brain or the subconscious mind as internal sources.

Interaction with higher thinkers might not be necessarily direct but could be through the medium of their written words, thoughts, speeches or spoken words, or researches. These external exposures give us thoughts we could meditate or muse upon, causing thought vibrations of rapid rate proportion to the height, in other context, depth, or creativeness of such thought. Long term or persistent engagement of the brain in this deliberate act of thinking increases the receptiveness of the brain to higher thought and increases the ability to understand very fast thought coming from the external environment or internal sources and because by nature, the brain is programmed to alter or adopt new experience, a point is reached when every thought stimulus sourced from any medium is vibrated at a very rapid rate above nominal, making all forms of thought coming from the brain productive.

The act of deliberate thinking may require you to decide first what to think about, sit and then think in an environment without distractions, write down what you hope to accomplish and take notes of what you think about.

a. Decide on what to think about
   As a Christian minster interacting with young people at various levels, when teaching on the "thought" subject. Many young individuals still ask what they should actually spend their time thinking about. Here are tips on what you can think about. Obviously, you might have to find what works for you and adjust things to fit your personal needs. But the following also, can be of help or give you an edge.
- Personal goals; identifying your potentials, your aspirations and how you can reach what you intend to achieve.
- How to get the most out of your current business
- How to add to your ability, competence or specialness
- Thinking wealthy
- Your career plans

b. No distractive environment
An environment with little or no distraction proves to be very helpful in focusing the brain on one thing and improving concentration. What may be pointed out, however, as a distraction may vary to different individual and depends on the height of thought. An environment full of distractions might be a coffee shop to someone working on coming up with a mathematical theorem, whereas to someone thinking of how to get the most out of his business, it is a distractive free environment.

c. Write down what you hope to accomplish.
You must write down on paper your plans, and what you intend to achieve or get out of any thinking process or session. It enables you to know at the end of the thinking session if you have accomplished what you set out to get from the session. For example, the written down plan could be about;
- How to market a product
- How to increase public awareness of a product
- 5 ways to earn more and work less

d. Taking note of thought
Writing down ideas, methodology, drawing diagrams help you clarify what you are thinking about and let you see the thinking process much more easily than when it is just in your head

3. WRITING

Isaiah 30:8 *"Now go, WRITE it before them in a table, and note it in* book that *it may be for the time to come forever and ever:"*

Jeremiah 30:2 "Thus *speaketh the Lord God of Israel, saying, WRITE thee all the words that I have spoken unto thee in a book."*

Habakkuk 2:2 *"And the Lord answered me, and said, WRITE the vision, and make it plain upon tables, that he may run that readeth it."*

2 Thessalonians 3:17 *"The salutation of Paul with mine own hand, which is the token in every epistle: SO I WRITE."*

1 John 1:4 *"And these things WRITE we unto you, that your joy may be full."*

Writing involves giving relative permanence to words or symbols recorded as a means of communication. It is an instrument for transmitting culture, preserving and transferring information and languages from generation to generation. The discipline of writing dates back to ancient humanity, more than 5000 years ago and according to the scriptural verses above, this discipline also passed down through the old and new testament period, with its advantage made used of, by God and His servants in bringing enlightenment and knowledge to humanity. However, the discipline of writing itself is one way in which we could upgrade the brain. This discipline that upgrades our brain does not work out by just recopying already existing information into another writing material, but involves getting thoughts from your faculty of creative or synthetic imagination onto a paper.

The imaginative faculty of man is the workshop where productive thoughts and ideas as thought stimuli are fashioned. Through the aid of this faculty, man has evolved from being primitive to being civilized and enlightened. By this faculty, man has birthed forth technology, discovered and harnessed more of nature's force to satisfy any of his need.

Therefore, the limitation of any man lies in his use and development of his imagination. Just as any muscle of the body develops through use, both the synthetic and creative faculties of imagination become more alert with use. High thinkers and successful individuals in any calling become what they are; great, because they develop the faculty of creative imagination. Writing is one major way we make use of and develop our creative imagination. Before thoughts are written down or documented, if the thought stimuli are coming from the faculty of imagination, the creative faculty becomes alerted and consequently allowed to function. Continuous alerting and functioning through use by practising, on a regular basis, the art of writing down your thoughts from this faculty, begins to develop this faculty until the brain grows to become very creatively imaginative.

Writing also makes your thought concrete and visible. It allows you to clarify what you are thinking and refine your idea. Writing makes you smarter because it forces you deeper into a subject and shows you areas of your subject that you do not fully understand.

If you have no clue to how to begin writing or what to write about, here are suggestions that might guide you to a start.

- Write during your devotions, meditate upon a particular verse of scripture, at least one and begin to write about a personal expanded view of what the studied verse might mean. Write to at least, one full page.
- Write about an interesting topic that pertains to your career. At least once per week
- You could create a personal blog which can cover pretty much any topic and give you a way to get your content up where others can benefit from it and interact with you.
- Join a teaching group in your local church which gives you a platform, where you could write about different things and share them with people.

Other benefits of writing
- Expressive writing involves putting down what you think and how you feel. Research on expressive writing has been able to link it with therapeutic benefits which include reducing stress levels, improving mood and bringing happiness to those who do it often.

Laura King in a research shows that, people who love writing about achieving future goals and dream become happier and healthier. Adam Grant and Jane Dutton also found out about writing that, when people who engage in

stressful fund raising jobs keep a journal for a few days about how their work made a difference, they increase their hourly effort by 29% over the next two weeks
- According to Gregory Ciotti, writing has a long term emotional benefit to people who experience traumatic events. In an old study he said, participants who write about traumatic events would actually become more depressed, until about six months, when the emotional benefits start to stick. In that study, one participant according to Ciotti, noted, "Although I have not talked with anyone about what I wrote, I was finally able to deal with it, work through the pain instead of trying to block it out. Now it doesn't hurt to think about it."
- More often, writing about the good things in your life motivates you about your presents and the future.
- Writing more often increases your ability to communicate effectively. It has even been shown to help people communicate highly complex ideas more effectively.
- Mastering the art of effective writing has birthed forth bestselling authors in the world today.

4. **ASSOCIATION**
   Proverb 13:20 *"He that walketh with wise men shall be wise: but a companion of fools shall be destroyed."*
   This verse of scripture is telling us that the kind of people we associate with (interact with on a frequent base, those who indoctrinate us with

their way of life, those we learn from, those we commune and fellowship with, those involved in teaching us, those who influence our belief system) play a major role in making us become a reflection of themselves. The process also works out in brain upgrade as our thinking pattern becomes a reflection of the people we closely associate with.

In order to upgrade your brain, you must associate with individuals who think very much higher than yourself. It occurs by listening to the words and watching the actions of these higher thinkers. Words and actions are end products of a thinking process, even supported by the scriptural verse which says *out of the abundance of the heart (mind; mentality), the mouth speaks*. These words and actions of higher thinkers that come to us every day are captured by the ears and eyes as external thought stimuli, they go to the thought creation centre of the brain to cause thought vibration of the same frequency with the vibrations of thought of higher thinkers.

The words and actions of higher thinkers when heard or sighted respectively also go to our subconscious mind to be stored, they go to our memory, and they activate our imaginative faculty or even influence our autosuggestions. As a result, our brain grows and becomes receptive to higher thinking. The brain does not only have more stored data and information that could be sources of internal thought stimuli, but engages in high frequency thought vibration every day due to the frequent interaction with high thinkers.

Higher thinkers also engage in new activities and experiences to keep themselves smarter. They believe that doing something new as frequent will keep them smart – fit. In consequence, associating with such higher thinkers allow you to consciously or unconsciously begin to seek out and do something new that is unusual to your routine. Such new experiences could be as simple as;

- Drawing
- Attending a lecture on a topic you know nothing about
- Watching documentaries
- Attending a city commission meeting
- Playing a smart game
- Spending few hours in municipal court as observer
- Driving through a new route
- Different kinds of body fitness exercises
- Attending an art display
- Going to a museum
- Learning a new language etc.

These activities would surely give your brain something new to think about and process. However they may actually not be life changing.

Platforms for associations

- Family platform

- Teacher-student platform
- Mentor-mentee platform
- Indirect associations
- Friend/colleague platform
- Master mind alliances.

5. MOTIVATION

Job 32:8 KJV "but there is a spirit in man, and the inspiration of the almighty giveth understanding."

The Encarta English dictionary gives a synonym of motivation to be the word inspiration, because of their very close relative meaning. In the context of the scriptural verse above, both the word inspiration and motivation could fit in without variance. Therefore the verse could be rephrased as "the motivation of the almighty giveth understanding"

Motivation is the reason for a person's behaviour or the cause of action or activities carried out by people. Man's behaviours typically are channelled towards meeting his needs. Such needs could be as those ranked by the American psychologist, Abraham Maslow; physiological needs, security and safety, love and feelings of belonging, competence, prestige and esteem, self fulfilment, curiosity and the need to understand.

Motivation which in humans could be conscious or unconscious drives man to behave in ways and manners that will ensure the satisfaction of his needs. The brain operates in like manner via its motivational system. The brain is programmed to behave in ways that ensure human survival and the satisfaction of needs or targeted goals. How the brain does this is that, it provides itself with certain goals (probably for success, wealth or excellence) and subsequently translates into a set of specific goal promoting behaviour that would drive him to meet those goals. The motivational system of the brain monitors the state of satisfaction of these goals, and activates behaviours necessary to meet needs that arise and drive the man in pursuit of attaining his brain set goals.

It is important to know what the motivational system of the brain does in order to fully understand what role it plays in the brain upgrading process.

All men, by nature, desire success and wealth, but in the world we live in, not all are focused enough to have definite set goals that would ultimately meet this desire. But for the brains that have adjusted to become focused enough, desirous and have set its success goals, the motivational system of the brain would now need to be excited more often, for it is by this system, proper behaviours are initiated (when excited) to drive that individual to his goals. The motivational system necessary to promote a goal only functions when it is excited. These excitements are not only positive such as praise but could be negative such as rage and anger. The motivational system may become weak, inactive or quiescent through lack of excitement.

Motivation also steps up vibrations of thoughts causing much more rapid vibration rate than it would, without motivation, and it also acts upon the forces of creative imagination. There are many other positive elements of excitement to motivation, but we shall examine or highlight few commonly used in creative effort.

- Faith
- Strong desire
- Enthusiasm
- Praise
- Love
- Sex

FAITH: This is one of the most powerful positive motivations. It steps up vibrations of thought and drives man into continually behaving or being convinced of eventual goal attainment. Faith is a conviction and state of mind induced by affirmation or repeated instruction through the principle of autosuggestion to the subconscious mind.

When you frequently send affirmation signals through autosuggestion to the subconscious mind, it acts on your belief system which it passes back to you in form of faith. This faith now excites the motivational system of the brain, allowing it to continually initiate behaviours or adopt a better behaviour that will accomplish your goals.

STRONG DESIRE: There is a state of mind that burns with strong desire for something, probably towards a set goal. The strong desire directly links up to the brain's motivation system. A strong desire TO BE and TO DO is the starting point of which goal pursuit must take off. Strong desire is like an inexhaustible fuel burning the train of motivation enhancing your persistence amidst various challenges.

PRAISE: This means expression of approval or admiration in words, recognition, award, acknowledgement, appreciation and commendation for someone's achievements or for something's good qualities.

It must be noted that the motivational system of the brain works also by a reward-punishment mechanism. The reward mechanism is activated, when a particular behaviour yields a favourable result. The reward mechanism induces structural process inside the brain that causes the same behaviour to be repeated subsequently whenever a similar situation arises.

Praises earned after attaining a favourable results activate the reward mechanism of the brain motivational system which causes the same behaviour to be repeated for more favourable results in the future.

LOVE: This is regarded as one of the most powerful emotions in the world. It creates a very high form of energy known to the mind of man. It is many a time expressed at the level of passions or else becomes transmuted into spiritual coin of real and lasting value. Love is the giving-ness of the self. It is expressed through the self-giving-ness of the lover to the object of his love. That is why, when we love people, we will go to the limit to help or serve them. Nothing is too great, no sacrifice is enough. The true lover gives all and is unhappy in not having still more of him to give to the object of his love.

The state of mind filled with love excites its motivational system, altering the behaviour of the lover to satisfy the needs of his object of love. It should be noted however, that in the context of upgrading the brain and achieving your goals, you must transmute the energy of love, focusing such energy at achieving your goals rather than only satisfying the desire of your object of love. For example, when your object of love desires that a particular goal of yours (not his/her or it) be achieved, of course, you will unapologetically focus your love energy at achieving that goal of yours in order to please your object of love.

It should not be misunderstood that the love we are talking about here is that expressed through sexual desire, because by our emotional nature, we may assume so. In Christianity, only the love kind called "agape" which expresses true love towards God and humanity (cutting across friends and families) is considered necessary and superior. Any other love, sexually expressed is meant for individuals legally bounded in MARRIAGE. Therefore, anyone that engages in sexual desires or relationship, thinking it is the expression of love will certainly enter into his/her destruction, for it depletes the vitality and demagnetizes the one who indulges in it. We must learn to love all people and not just some people.

SEX: In Christianity, the subject of sex is a very sensitive one and must not be misunderstood. Note also that indulging in sex outside marriage or prematurely is wrong and can lead to one's destruction. Sexual relationship is meant and ONLY meant for legally married individuals. My aim in this section is not to promote the subject of sex but to expose the possibilities of its constructive potentialities that can be harnessed by "married couples" in upgrading their brains and living a higher life. Sex (done in the legal way) has its spiritual implications (unionism), biological implication (reproduction) and physical implications (maintenance of health). But beyond this, it has its mental implications.

Sex desire is the most powerful of human desires, for men have even risked their lives and reputation just to indulge in sexual contact. Men have been robbed of their fortunes because of certain traits of sexual desire and sexual pursuit. Top among the root cause of this is man's inability or unwillingness to teem his "SELF" and the energy of his sexual emotion. Not to forget that he has not understood how to transmute that desire and energy to some other forms of desire and action that can lift one to become a higher thinker.

When driven by sexual desire, man's thought vibrations are keyed up to a very high rate, they develop keenness to imagination and creative abilities. Sexual desires excite the brain motivational system even uncontrollably; they therefore require much teeming or transmutation.

Since we know that higher thinkers are made when they have discovered how to increase their thought vibrations which turn every nominal thought stimulus coming from either the external or internal environment into a creative form of thought not available through the ordinary rate of vibration of thought. Amongst the greatest and most powerful emotions or stimuli that shot up vibrations of thought is the sex energy. However, the possession of this energy is not sufficient to produce higher thinkers. The energy must be harnessed and transmuted by deliberate will power into higher thinking of making humanity better.

BRAIN MOTIVATIONAL LANGUAGE

This speaks of the manner of motivation that excites the brain the most. People have different brain motivational languages. What would have excited to a higher degree one's brain motivational system maybe unexciting to another's. Discovering your brain motivational language is essential if you are to keep your mind on high vibrations always.

I graduated from high school as the best student in physics. I came to love and got obsessed with physics because of the praises of my physics teacher. He would always praise me before my fellow mates in class, telling them of how proud he was of me and that he believed that no one in the same class could beat me in physics. So in order for my teacher's praises not to become a past glory, I increased my effort to study physics so much more until it became an inherent part of me.

What my physics teacher did, maybe without his knowledge was activating my brain motivational system; commendation. This gave me an edge to fall in love with physics and turning me into a genius.

Having heard the various brain excitement activators (praise, faith, love, enthusiasm, strong desire, sex, others may include, promises, gifts etc.), you must identify your brain motivational language. What makes you feel very happy and excited? What brings out the best in you? What makes you feel loved and fulfilled?

What brings you on? Your answers to this question are the key to discovering what can take your mind to the highest plane of thoughts. If the answer to these questions does not leap to your mind immediately, perhaps the following approaches may be of help to discovering your motivational language.

Examine what you do or say always in motivating people. Chances are that what you are doing or saying to others in order to motivate them is what you desire to be motivated with. Then, that may be your motivational language.

Another way to discover your motivational language is to examine what it is that others do or fail to do to you that hurt you most deeply. Chances also are that the opposite of what hurts you most is probably your brain motivational language.

What makes you sit and think deeply on what could make you great? Chances also are that that attitude may be keeping in resultant effect to a brain motivation. Another approach is to look back also overtime and examine what attitude of people lightens up your emotions, because that may probably be in keeping with your motivational language.

But note that approach is only a possible clue to your brain motivation language, it is not an absolute indicator and it is also possible to have more than one brain motivational language. It also still lies upon you to discover that situation, action, words and attitude in which if experienced gives you an edge to becoming creative in thought. You must use every opportunity of motivation and excitement to sit and think of possible solutions to problems or idea creation, for at this point the mind has been stimulated for higher thinking.

NUTRITION:

1KINGS 19:8

"And he arose, and did eat and drink and went in the strength of that meat forty days and forty night........"

The bible in this verse tells us that bodily strength is sourced from food (nutrition), in like case also, the brain.

Human nutrition studies how foods affect the health and survival of the human body, likewise brain nutrition, the functioning and efficiency of the human brain. The human brain is always "ON" and it works 24 hours without pause. The implication is that the brain would require a continuous supply of energy which can only come from food. However what makes up the food that gives the brain its fuel to function makes all the difference, because the kinds of food we eat directly affect the structure and function of the brain.

The brain functions best when supplied with the right kind of fuel. Best brain functioning is required for proper high thinking and memory efficiency. Eating high quality foods that contain vitamins, minerals, and antioxidants nourish the brain and protect it from oxidative stress.

Brain upgrade might not be possible using the biblical supported scientific strategies highlighted except given the best conditions to occur. There are brain power foods that do not only create these proper conditions or maintain good brain health but boost, upgrade or improve cognitive and mental health. Research has shown also that individuals can increase their chances of maintaining a healthy brain well into old age if they add these brain power foods into their daily eating regimen.

These brain power foods can turn your diet from one that does little for your brain to one that can really boost your mental quality.

- Fishes such as wildly caught fishes, wild salmon, herring, mackerel, sardines etc. are excellent in omega-3 fat DHA. DHA is a major building block of the brain. Findings have shown that people low in DHA actually have smaller brains that age faster than those with normal levels.
- Blue berries are very good fruits. They help protect the brain from oxidative stress and may reduce the risk of Alzheimer's disease or dementia
  Dementia: progressive deterioration with age of intellectual function such as memory.
  Alzheimer's disease: progressive brain disorder resulting in decline in memory, cognition and even consequently the inability to care for oneself.
  - Coconut and extra virgin olive oil; they are better for overall healthy state. Coconut is a brain power food because of its medium chain triglycerides (MCTs) which bypasses glucose metabolism, delivering energy

straight to the brain cells. Coconut oil according to nutritional psychiatrics is effective for depression, memory decline and the effect of brain aging. Extra virgin olive oil itself is high in brain protective vitamin E, vitamin K and polyphenols.

- Nuts and seeds such as walnuts, hazelnuts, brazil nuts, filberts, almonds, cashew, peanuts, sunflower seeds, sesame seeds, flax seed are all good sources of vitamin E. Steven Pratt, author of *"Superfood Rx: fourteen foods proven to change your life"* establishes that higher levels of vitamin E correspond with less cognitive decline as you get older. He also identifies that avocado which is a fatty food is a good contributor to healthy blood flow; lower blood pressure. And since hypertension is a risk factor for the decline in cognitive abilities, a lower blood pressure would promote brain health.
- Good quality chocolates increase blood flow to the brain, protect the brain from free radical damage and lower the risk of dementia. It is a source of anandamide, a neurotransmitter known as the "bliss molecule". Chocolate also improves memory, learning and concentration. Ancient Aztecs used to drink bitter chocolate with cinnamon and vanilla for a treat. This mixture is excellent in satisfying cravings for chocolate while promoting brain health.

Extra tips: how to prepare the mixture
Ingredient:
Milk (low fat)
Cinnamon sticks
Bittersweet dark chocolate (chopped)
Vanilla extract
Pinch salt
Sugar (2 spoons)
Preparation:
- In a saucepan, put your milk and cinnamon sticks and boil a little.
- Allow to sit for 45 minutes to 2 hours to fill the milk with cinnamon flavour.
- Then remove cinnamon stick. Add sugar, salt and vanilla.
- Return milk to boil, where you put in your chopped chocolate at low heat.
- Once chocolate is melted, put in a cup and serve warm

- Turmeric has its active ingredient as Curcumin. Curcumin is a potent antioxidant that readily crosses the blood brain barrier to protect your brain from free radical damage. Turmeric can improve memory, concentration, brain cell products, production of serotonin and dopamine. It is known also to reduce the risk of brain inflammation, Alzheimer's disease etc.
- Spices such as ginger, cinnamon, black pepper, curry garlic, saffron are known to improve brain function and protect it from early aging.

- Herbs such as basil, chives, oregano, parsley, rosemary, sage and thyme are known with significant brain boosting power. Carnosic acid contained in rosemary protects the brain from strokes and neurodegenerative diseases.
- Nutraceuticals; these are nutrients that are usually compound made by the body or are plant based. They are known to have specific medicinal or pharmacological effect. They can be effective brain enhancers. Examples include; Acetyl-L- carnitine, krill oil or upgraded coffee.

SPIRITUALITY

Matthew 19:26 "...but with God all things are possible..."

Spirituality is a non-negotiable key to upgrading the brain. Although we know that the brain organ takes a material, natural form, however it is also an established fact that the real man is actually immaterial. That is to say, man is a spirit; he has also a soul and lives in a body. Here is one simple way to understand the man-nature. Man has a material part, the body and an immaterial part, which are the soul and the spirit. Some individuals view the man nature as a bipartite, where the soul and the spirit are taken as only different terms for the same entity. However, greater number of theologians and bible teachers hold on to a more reliable view of the tripartite nature of man, suggesting that man's immaterial nature has two distinctly different parts of the spirit and soul.

God, the highest thinker, most impossible to understand is a spirit and by his wisdom created man as a very complex being having these three entities that are interconnected. The spirit-soul part of man can never be destroyed and is in a condition of infinite perfection; it is also superior to and dominates over the material body. It is universally esteemed more valuable than the material in its most beautiful state. The superiority of the spirit-soul part of man is not only apparent over the body, but over a nature that combines the spirit, soul and body. That is to say, the material nature of man is inferior to the spiritual and it is controlled by it. It is also imperfect and has an inherent tendency to diminish.

It is by our body that we function and have a physical form on this material realm, connecting to it with our five senses. The soul gives us our personality. It is believed to be made up of the will and emotions of man and also as part of him where the mind of man is constructed. The spirit however gives meaning to man's life. It is through the spirit that man also communicates and relates with the immaterial realm. It is through the spirit that man has communion and fellowship with God. It is therefore on the platform of spirituality that man can associate and interact with the highest thinker, who enlightens the spirit-soul part of man, consequently causing the mentality, thoughts and the total brain of the material man to be upgraded.

John 4:24 *"God is spirit and they that worship him must worship him in spirit and in truth."*

This verse of scripture signifies that intimate union between the divine spirit and his intelligent creation is only founded on spiritual bases.

The word spirituality sometimes can be misused in a different concept since the immaterial realm is made up of the divine life (God) and other evil forces. But the Christian concept and view of spirituality is the key to upgrading the brain. This view suggests spirituality as an indication of man being regenerated, indwelt, enlightened, endued, empowered and guided by the Holy Spirit, conformed to the will of God, having the mind of Christ, living in and led by the spirit. Being spiritual affords the state of a man's soul which covers the entire range of his faculties; reasoning, thinking, intellect, emotions, beliefs, memories or choices to be vitalized by the divine spirit and made alive unto God.

The greatest definition of spirituality in the Christian context is God likeness, which involves developing and growing in the nature of God. From creation, God desires to make man someone he can be able to relate with, and so man was made with the capabilities of being spiritual for proper relationship with God who himself is spirit. Spirituality therefore in another Christian-viewed definition is relationship with God (the highest thinker).

We associate with the highest thinker by various mediums that spiritually transcend the material nature of man;

- Revolutionizing the belief system of the mind by adopting a system of belief endorsed by the highest thinker;
- Reading and meditating the thoughts of the highest thinker (the word of God);
- Prayer; a medium of communication with the highest thinker;
- Change from the sinful nature to the redeemed nature of man;
- Outpouring, infilling, indwelling of the holy spirit in the spiritual nature of man, with wilful submission to the holy spirit;
- Strong desire and love for to associate with God; and
- Total obedience to the standards of God.

Total brain upgrade goes beyond upgrading the mentality and productivity of the material man. It also upgrades man's immaterial nature. No man is totally and truly a genius except he or she is also spiritually intelligent.

Spirituality (associating with the highest thinker) benefits man in four major areas of interest to us;

- Spiritual intelligence
- Wisdom
- The anointing
- Wealth

SPIRITUAL INTELLIGENCE; unlike natural intelligence, this deals with the knowledge and understanding of information (mysteries) that are only spiritually discernible. It is the ability to;

- Discern the mysteries of the scriptures.
- Think and understand the thoughts of the highest thinker.
- Gain scriptural insights and accurately analyse them.
- Understand by visions and revelations (supernatural enlightenment of the mind to the extent of creating supernatural images in the mind whether in consciousness or sub-consciousness).
- Understand by hearing directly the voice of God (the highest thinker) - this is an ability given to the spiritually upgraded and redeemed nature of man.
- Spiritually discern cause and effects, times, seasons, thoughts, actions etc.

WISDOM:

James 3: 15-17 *"This wisdom descendeth not from above, but is earthly, sensual, devilish. For where envying and strife is, there is confusion and every evil work. But the wisdom that is from above is first pure, then peaceable, gentle, and easy to be intreated, full of mercy and GOOD FRUITS (that means; productive), without partiality, and without hypocrisy".*

The Bible tells us that there is a wisdom known as spiritual wisdom that comes from associating with God. This wisdom gives one the ability to judge and make a true estimate of things, persons, times, and events. This wisdom also directs to the right end, such as may be perfective of our nature and is a necessary virtue needed for the Christian – management of affairs, success and safety. While some individuals believe that this wisdom, for the nature and substance of it, is a duty and obligation of a Christian, others suggest it to be a gift. However, a more reliable truth is that whether wisdom is a gift, privilege or duty, it cannot be attained except in spiritual mindedness (state of being spiritual – state of being in communion with God).

THE ANOINTING

The greatest privilege granted to man at redemption was the capacity to be indwelt by the spirit of God (the highest thinker). The Bible then records in Isaiah11:2-3 that the spirit of God expresses Himself in man's physical nature as what is known as the anointing. The anointing is of several kinds and distinctions, but in the context of brain upgrade, the anointing of knowledge and that of understanding is of the most importance as the Bible itself admonishes in Proverbs 4:7 that wisdom is the principal thing; therefore get wisdom and in all your getting, get understanding.

The anointing grants man the supernatural abilities and possibilities of doing things not natural to his state. This is also a reward of spiritual mindedness.

WEALTH

Deuteronomy 8:*18 "But thou shalt remember the Lord thy God: for it is he that giveth thee power to get wealth,..."*

Some of history's joyous stories consist of men and women alike whose spiritual mindedness granted them access to great wealth. Certainly wealth is an effect of possessing supernatural wisdom, spiritual intelligence and the anointing. But the greatest power to getting wealth is in the knowledge of a *"special secret"*, which can be only known spiritually and by association with the highest thinker.

SPIRITUAL MEANS TO UPGRADING THE BRAIN:

The word: "logos" is the Greek word to represent the "word" of God, which means the thoughts of God. The word of God gives you God's ideologies and the contents of his thought patterns. By reading and meditating these written words, you are brought into the study of his ideas, instructions and desires. Staying long with His words alongside opening up yourself to the influence of His thought patterns, you will begin to think like the highest thinker. The word of God transcends to a force that compels the mind to align to spiritual things. The spiritually intelligent man is one whose ideologies are a derivative of the word of God rather than circumstances, culture and the society.

Prayer: proper biblical praying is a two way communication between man and God, the highest thinker (2 Corinthians 12:8-9). That means as you talk to God, you must learn to get a feedback from him. The results of getting a feedback from God is access to ideas, wisdom, revelations, hunches, or creative words that are not common to man's natural thoughts.

Prayers also engage the indwelling spirit of God in man's immaterial nature to stimulate the faculty of creative imagination to become receptive to ideas coming from the spirit of the Lord.

The Bible affirms to us again in James 1:5 that wisdom can be attained through deliberate prayers as a gift from God's reward system.

The Spirit of the Lord: the spirit indwelt the natural man makes the redeemed man, while the spirit in-filled the natural man makes the anointed man. The Holy Spirit is able to infill a natural man, turning him to an extraordinary thinker.

The Holy Spirit;

- Inspires (2 Timothy 3:16)
- Motivates (Job 32:8)
- Reveals secret (Daniel 2:28)
- Stimulates the creative imagination (Exodus 31:2)
- Step up vibrations of thoughts

Open heaven:

Malachi 3:*10 "Bring ye all the tithes into the storehouse, that there may be meat in mine house, and prove me now herewith, saith the Lord of hosts, if I will not open you the windows of heaven, and pour you out a blessing, that there shall not be room enough to receive it."*

Deuteronomy 28:23 "And thy heaven that is over thy head shall be brass, and the earth that is under thee shall be iron."

The Bible confirms to us from this verse of scripture that onto every man, a particular airspace known as his heaven has been appointed to him spiritually, just as spiritual heavens are over our cities, nations and the world at large. This heaven may be closed or opened spiritually and the state of your heaven whether closed or opened determines your success, wealth and the height of your thoughts.

The implication of a closed heaven which may be caused by sin, disobedience, limited, incomplete or no tithing is that it leads to stagnancy of the mind, consequently, little or no ideas, scarcity of productiveness, baseline thinking, lack of inspiration and motivation, spiritual and intellectual dullness and then ultimately poverty.

Open heaven on the opposite hand, which gives a free way access of communion with the highest thinker leads to productivity of the mind and body.

Tithing opens your heavens;

Tithing does not directly give you wealth as thought by most people. Tithing is only a spiritual law which enforces open heavens when consistently obeyed and applied. Obeying the law of tithing allows your work and brain to operate under open heavens, with ease, favour, effortless, inspiring, creative, and productive and then ultimately increasing your wealth index.

THE GREATEST BIBLICAL SECRET OF WEALTH

Wealth comes to you when you produce more results. But results are not accidental; they are the product of working the principles of God's system. Wealth, as likewise anything of great value, is not free. There is always a cause to an effect and a "DOING" before an "ACQUIRING"

Matthew 19:**16** *"And, behold, one came and said unto him, Good Master, what good thing* **shall I DO,** *that I may have eternal life?"*

From this verse, the mindset of a wealthy man was unveiled to us who understand that results do not just occur (even salvation), but are the products of first**,** ***a Doing***. But what must you do in the kingdom to be wealthy?

In the kingdom, the first thing to do to become wealthy is to thrive to know the secrets of wealth. This secret is no secret but having access to and understanding the secrets of the lord.

The secrets of the Lord and the knowing of these secrets are the secret of achieving results and wealth in life. David in the bible revealed this, as his testimony of how he accomplished great exploits and wealth in Psalm 24:15.

Psalm 25:14 *"The secret of the Lord is with them that fear him; And he will show them his covenant."*

In the system of God's kingdom, there are secrets to every kind of results and even wealth that all men desire. Although these secrets are worthy of being revealed but only to those who fear the Lord. In God's kingdom, there is the secret of longevity, the secret of wealth, the secret of power, the secret of the anointing, the secret of the presence of God and so on. Knowing any of these secrets and applying the revealed knowledge will certainly produce the corresponding results. Job also attributed the so many results in his life to knowledge of the secrets of the lord.

Job 29:4-25

Verse 4: As I was in the days of my youth, when **THE SECRET OF GOD** *was upon my tabernacle,*

Verse 5: When the Almighty was yet with me, when my children were about me,

Verse 6: When I washed my steps with butter, **(WEALTH)** *and the rock poured me out rivers of oil;* **(THE ANOINTING)**

Verse 7: When I went out to the gate through the city, when I prepared my seat in the street!

Verse 8: The young men saw me, and hid themselves: and the aged arose, and stood up **(HONOUR);**

Verse 9: The princes refrained talking, and laid their hand on their mouth **(REVERANCE;**

Verse 10: The nobles held their peace, and their tongue cleaved to the roof of their mouth.

Verse 11: When the ear heard me, then it blessed me; and when the eye saw me, it gave witness to me:

Verse 12: Because I delivered the poor that cried, and the fatherless, and him that had none to help him **(the secret teaches how to LOVE)**.

Verse 13: The blessing of him that was ready to perish came upon me: and I caused the widow's heart to sing for joy.

Verse 14: I put on righteousness, and it clothed me **(RIGHTEOUSNESS):** *my judgment was as a robe and a diadem.*

Verse 15: I was eyes to the blind, and feet was I to the lame.

Verse 16: I was a father to the poor: and the cause which I knew not I searched out. **(WISDOM)**

Verse 17: And I broke the jaws of the wicked, and plucked the spoil out of his teeth **(POWER)**.

Verse 18: Then I said, I shall die in my nest, and I shall multiply my days as the sand **(LONGEVITY AND PEACE)**.

Verse 19: My root was spread out by the waters, and the dew lay all night upon my branch **(BLESSINGS)**.

Verse 20: My glory was fresh in me, and my bow was renewed in my hand **(GLORY AND STRENGTH)**.

Verse 21: Unto me men gave ear, and waited, and kept silence at my counsel **(WISDOM)**.

Verse 22: After my words they spake not again; and my speech dropped upon them.

*Verse 23: And they waited for me as for the rain; and they opened their mouth wide as for the latter rain (**INDISPENSABLE**).*

Verse 24: If I laughed on them, they believed it not; and the light of my countenance they cast not down.

*Verse 25: I chose out their way, and sat chief, and dwelt as a king in the army, as one that comforteth the mourners (**AUTHORITY**).*

All these results are the product of his knowledge of the secrets of God.

CHAPTER SIX: GENIUS

Do you desire to be a genius?

The difference between a genius and an ordinary thinker or man is that the genius relies and makes demands upon the sixth sense for the generation of his thought creation stimuli while an ordinary thinker is largely guided by thought creation stimuli generated from his memory where he accumulates experiences. However, not all the experiences and knowledge we accumulate over time are totally accurate or extraordinary enough, but anything received through a healthy sixth sense are much more reliable because they come from sources more reliable than any which generates thought stimuli to the brain.

Genii are made through the deliberate and purposeful use of the sixth sense. The Encarta English dictionary referred the sixth sense to be a source of various intuitions and hunches, a supposedly extra sense having the ability to perceive something not using any of the five senses of sight, hearing, touch, smell and taste. Napoleon Hill in his book, 'Think and Grow Rich' affirms to his readers of the availability of many reliable evidences that establish the reality of the sixth sense through the analysis of men who have become successful and great although having no extensive lifelong education but have discovered, developed and made use of their sixth sense.

This sixth sense is creative imagination or the creative faculty. It is however saddening that only a little fraction of individuals during their entire life time, discovered, fully developed and with understanding, deliberately and purposefully used their faculty of creative imagination to become successful or outstanding. Those who truly have, are actually the ones known as genius.

Creative imagination links the limited mind of man, his subconscious mind and unlimited or infinite intelligence. When developed through constant use and reliance upon its faculty, creative imagination can be an excellent source of powerful, creative and higher thoughts. The faculty of creative imaginations draws upon the immaterial forces, elements or vibrations sourced from the following and its acts upon them to produce ideas, concepts, intuition or hunches received as higher thoughts.

1. The subconscious mind
2. Infinite intelligence
3. Through the conscious thoughts of other people
4. Subconscious ideas as words or action coming from other people's subconscious faculty
5. Supernatural intelligence (religious view)

How the creative faculty functions best

The creative faculty not only develops through use, but also functions best during the process of higher thinking. Previous chapters have tried explaining how one can be able to step higher on his thinking by stepping up his vibrations of thought through

- Emotions and motivations
- Brain motivational system
- Brain reward mechanism
- Interactions with higher thinkers

- Supernatural elevations of thought vibrations

When the centre of reasoning or thought creation is vibrated with higher thoughts, the creative faculty is then given a good platform for expression. Higher thinking clears the way for the sixth sense to function and operate. It becomes very receptive to vibrations of ideas which could not reach the individual under any circumstances other than the higher thinking process.

During higher thinking, the creative imagination becomes alert and receptive to the immaterial force, elements or vibrations needed to produce ideas or hunches transmitting from either the individual's subconscious mind or the conscious and or subconscious mind of other people around.

How to develop the creative imagination

The creative faculty is developed only through constant use. The deliberate act of using the creative faculty with the purpose of becoming a genius (extraordinarily creative) would require you to do the following;

- Rely upon this faculty; you must be aware that every man has a sixth sense whether developed or not, and that you can rely and draw from it for any needed thought stimulus.
- Make demands upon it; this faculty can also be a source of internal thought stimuli, therefore, you must learn how to rely and make demand upon it for your thoughts rather than from the memory or experiences.

- You must continually practise how to step up the vibrations of your thoughts by using any of the procedure learned.
- You must know how to stimulate this faculty using the motivational system and reward mechanism of the brain.
- Before this faculty becomes developed at least to a greater extent, you must make use of it by concentration. That is to say, for example, you can paint a picture of your goal or what you desire in your mind and hold it there until it has been taken over by the subconscious mind, then clear your mind of all other thoughts and activities and concentrate on getting answers on how to produce your goal or desire.
- You must use, reuse and use; sometimes, depending upon the state of development of the creative faculty, the answers or results given from the faculty might be negative, partial or negligible, however you must never stop relying and making use of it until the positive results produced by it becomes consistent.

Creative imagination and the Anointing

The manifestation of the spirit of God usually comes as an expression of the anointing. The Bible tells us that the spirit of God expresses himself in man's material nature as seven dimensions or the expressions of the anointing as highlighted in Isaiah 11: 2-3.

Isaiah 11:2-3 *"And the spirit of the Lord shall rest upon him, the spirit of wisdom and understanding, the spirit of counsel and might, the spirit of knowledge and of the fear of the Lord; And shall make him of quick understanding in the fear of the Lord: and he shall not judge after the sight of his eyes, neither reprove after the hearing of his ears:"*

- *The anointing of wisdom*
- *The anointing of understanding*
- *The anointing of dominion (the spirit of the lord)*
- *The anointing of counsel*
- *The anointing of might*
- *The anointing of knowledge*
- *The anointing of the fear of the Lord*

The anointing as clearly signified in verse three is said to be able to make one of quick understanding in the fear of the Lord.

Exodus 31:2

"See, I have called by name Bezaleel the son of Uri, the son of Hur, of the tribe of Judah: And I have filled him with the spirit of God, in wisdom, and in understanding, and in knowledge, and in all manner of workmanship, To devise cunning works, to work in gold, and in silver, and in brass, And in cutting of stones, to set them, and in carving of timber, to work in all manner of workmanship."

The anointing has the capacity to supernaturally stimulate the faculty of creative imagination of the mind to become receptive to those revelations (supernatural "knowing") referred to in the realm of religion or to creative ideas coming from the spirit of God.

CHAPTER SEVEN: HEAD ATTACKERS

Genesis 3:15b ESV "...he shall bruise your HEAD and you shall bruise his heel..."
Genesis 3:15 GNB "...her offspring will crush your HEAD and you shall bruise his heel..."

The word "attack" can be used in various contexts. But generally it is used to mean; bruise, crush, damage, infect, criticize, cause harm, destroy, or to reduce efficiency etc.

The word "head" occurred in the Bible more than three hundred times. Most of those verses having the word "head" would however have had a better contextual meaning if it had been replaced with the word "brain".

For example:

Daniel 2:28 *"But there is a God in heaven that revealeth secrets, and maketh known to the king Nebuchadnezzar what shall be in the latter days. Thy dream, and the visions of thy head (**CONCEPTIONS FORMED IN THE BRAIN**) upon thy bed...;"*- Jamieson, Fausset, and Brown's Commentary of the Bible

However, the word "brain" came into existence few centuries back derived from the old English word "brægan" and so the old Bible writers had to use the word "head" as a representation of an organ that carries out intellectual functioning and body control in place of the word "brain". However, the head itself is of both

physical and spiritual importance in human life and existence. The material or natural man has seventy percent of his head space filled up with brain tissue and so therefore the brain is literally what makes up the head. The head, spiritually or in man's immaterial nature, connotes;
- The glory of man
- The totality of man's life
- The major form that contains man's greatness
- A collector of good and or evil
- The medium of spiritual influence to the body.
- Man's spiritual centre of communication
- Man's carriage centre for the anointing.
- Man's symbol of power and authority

Both God and other forces of the immaterial world, even with some humans who are in strong allegiance to Satan have always been interested in the issues that have to do with the head of man. This is because the head (brain) dictates the boundaries of man's intellectual capacity, determines how he rises above challenges, determines his willingness, actions, thoughts and decisions whether they are in alignment to God's standard or Satan's desire. The head (brain) determines the heights of man's achievement by his ability to imagine. The head is the centre of man's spiritual and natural intelligence. It is man's greatest asset.

A non arguable truth is that there are however powers, forces or personalities that attack the head, both physically and spiritually. Dark forces of the immaterial world, known as the head attackers, agents with strong allegiance to Satan, of which they have no desire to see man make use of the full potentials of his head (brain) to profit God and humanity. They desire and aim to ensure that man's capabilities, possibilities and potentials that can be harnessed from using the head (brain) remains hidden to man. They attack the head (brain) to keep man spiritually ignorant, they attack the head (brain) to negatively affect man's total health. Every attack on the head will also certainly run through one's total life, family, career, business etc. Every negative occurrence in history (most likely orchestrated by Satan) such as the brutal wars and revolutions leading to the loss of lives of millions of people (the holocaust, world wars) were the result of man's thinking, reasoning or imagination influenced by dark forces of immaterial or sometimes material nature.

These forces are able to affect the brain of man's material nature by influencing the head of the immaterial man, since the immaterial nature of man controls totally his material nature.

Head attackers could be immaterial forces or powers of the dark world or they could be wicked natural personalities of our material world that attack the capabilities and potentials of the brain, mind or head spiritually. Head attackers are spirits responsible for the lifelong baseline thinking patterns that have become strong holds in the lives of individuals. They are responsible for the constant irrational thoughts, behaviours and the unprofitable lifestyles of some people. The madness spirit is a head attacker. All forms of mentality and egos in man that rebel against God are sponsored by the head attackers.

Head attackers are the poverty spirit, vagabond spirit, and anti-excellent spirit, spirit of wastage, spirit of unproductiveness, spirit of laziness, and spirit of negative imaginations. These immaterial forces are given these names due to the nature of their manifestations. The Bible itself proves to us that the head had since been a prime target of attack by the enemy (Satan and his forces).

> *Psalm 7:16 "His mischief shall return upon his own head, and his violent dealing shall come down upon his own pate."*

For they know that by attacking the head (brain) of man, the following could occur; these are the various evidences or symptoms of head attacks;

- Constant confusion
- Suicidal thoughts and tendencies
- Madness
- Unusual loss of consciousness
- Constant negative emotions
- Constant negative thoughts
- Constant forgetfulness
- Frequent mind blankness
- Uncontrollable sexual desires
- Periodic irrational behaviours and words
- Poor concentration
- Stronghold baseline thinking
- Constant fear
- Sleeplessness
- Uncontrollable appetite for anything (Example: food)
- Unusual nausea
- Constant disorganisation
- Careless mistakes
- Restlessness

Higher Thoughts

- Excessive fantasy-dreams
- No desires, no aspirations and no goal
- Constant indecisions
- Unable to take the most little form of risk
- Drug addiction
- Excessive talking
- Memory problems
- Head heaviness
- Total un-creativeness
- Poor brain processing
- Poor brain recollections
- Total lack of wisdom
- Predicting the worst in life
- Irrational imaginations
- Unconscious masturbation
- Violation of argumentation
- Head bewitchment
- Vagabond lifestyle
- Excessive quietness
- Excessive sleep
- Excessive usage of vulgar languages
- Strong poverty mentality
- Reading difficulties
- Unconscious misbehaviours
- Disfavours
- Uncontrollable self centeredness
- Constant childish reasoning
- Uncontrollable lust and masturbations
- Uncontrollable rape thoughts
- Hearing of imaginary strange voices
- Absence of motivation

- Extreme bad emotions
- Tendency to expect the worst
- Total isolation
- Self inflicted physical abuse
- Tendency to abuse others sexually
- Homosexual preferences
- Obsessions with immoral dressings
- Short attention span
- Low energy
- Extreme anger
- Poor time and money management
- Extreme fear in darkness
- Negative belief systems
- Strong belief in all kinds of superstitions
- Poor judgement
- Depression at all times
- Abnormal laughter
- Poor attention
- Abnormal expression of emotions
- Lesbianism
- Frequent headaches
- Fear of doing something crazy
- Sexual looseness
- Headaches at every deep thought
- Inability to plan
- Lack of forward thinking
- Inability to express feelings
- Excessive day dreaming
- Practice of magic
- Total impatience
- Unexplainable hatred toward others

- Hallucinations
- Fear of shadows
- Investing money on unprofitable game playing
- Smoking
- Mental retardation
- Lack of common sense
- Lack of natural intelligence
- Lack of spiritual intelligence
- Total cowardice
- Extreme dirtiness
- Atheism
- Extremely negative temperament
- Total indiscipline of thoughts
- Dullness
- Brain retardation
- Constant anxiety
- Too late personality
- Partial madness
- Periodic madness
- Senselessness
- Serious academic failure
- Extreme emotional instability
- Deep lust
- Shame
- Bad habits
- Anti-excellence syndrome
- Insensitivity
- Inability to profit from experience
- Mental slowness
- Lacking keenness to perception
- Sexually deviant tendencies

- Extreme cruelty
- Fear (afraid of everyone)
- Resentment to wealth
- Maliciousness
- Mediocrity
- Outright criticality of others
- Entitlement mentality
- Inability to keep profitable relationships
- Lack of prudence
- Foolishness
- Procrastinations
- Costly errors
- Wrong direction
- Repeated tragedy
- Inability to make the right decisions
- Finishing fever; doing so many things at the same time but unable to successfully complete any.

These dark forces of immaterial nature have access to the Soulish realm of man, when he is in a state of vulnerability. The soulish realm is the centre of man's mentality, here; they influence one's autosuggestions by providing false information to suggest to oneself. They could influence also one's imaginations, sub-consciousness and go as far as affecting one's consciousness.

It will be unreasonable to conclude that the totality of man's life is affected only by elements of science, biology and intellectualism. It will also be unwise to neglect the fact that man has an immaterial nature, and that what happens to the natural man is dependent on the circumstances that affect his spirit man.

If you desire total brain upgrade, then you must deal with head attackers because you can be an intellectual genius but still be spiritually head attacked with madness. These attackers have thereby rendered one's genius useless.

Head attackers range from glory exchangers and traders (responsible for exchanging the potentialities and distinctive abilities of a man with something else of no profit.) to head burdeners (responsible for head heaviness, restlessness, sleeplessness, reading difficulties, memory problems), head manipulators (they negatively influence the thoughts, actions, habit, attitude, decision or behaviours of man, whether consciously or unconsciously.) or head bewitchers (using spells to place the head under powerful influence or strong fascination) and polluters and the spirit of death (responsible for total brain and body attack).

HOW THE DEVIL INFLUENCES YOUR THOUGHTS

The devil can access the mind of man especially at his most vulnerable state. The devil goes to the autosuggestion of the mind, where he puts in negative data that then runs as internal thought creation stimuli to the centre of thought creation where they are vibrated to become thoughts.

These thoughts now created can do so many things. They can go to the subconscious mind, be discarded or accepted to go to the place of memory storage, and it can still create a neural pathway connecting to the basal ganglia when these thoughts become persistent. We now know what happens in the basal ganglia, this is where habits would eventually be formed. Decisions can also be immediately made from these thoughts and consequently, actions are carried out.

FREEDOM FROM HEAD ATTACKERS

God has placed in man the ability to think high and be very creative. It is in these possibilities that man could become a genius or grow into his wealth. The agency of head attackers has only been established as a result of our evil world system and the sinful nature of the fallen man to ensure that these possibilities are not harnessed.

If you recognize that you are experiencing any of the symptoms of head attacks listed above, then what you need most and now is freedom from these attackers. Freedom from head attackers entails that you engage in the ministry of head deliverance.

One very essential and compulsory weapon necessary to engage the ministry of head deliverance is prayer. Remember, head attackers target the spiritual or immaterial nature of man, and so then freedom also must be sought after and attained spiritually. Prayer is arguably the most important weapon of spiritual warfare available to the redeemed man. Prayer is a force and medium of communication that transcends the material to the immaterial. It is a defensive and offensive weapon, and a means of communication to God. It provokes God to action and disengages, disarm head attackers. Prayer is both the master key to both spiritual victory and freedom.

BEFORE YOU PRAY!

Do you want to pray now? Oh! Good! But hold on;
It is important that while you prepare to engage the ministry of head deliverance or attack head attackers through prayers, you should first ask yourself the following questions because answers to your prayers depend solemnly on how correct and true your answers are to these questions;

- Am I a Christian? If yes
- Am I born again? If no, repent now! But if you claim you are, continue then!
- Am I true with God? Or am I a pretender, a hypocrite?
- If I were God, would I listen to my prayers?
- Are my prayers weighted with sincere desire and soaked in faith and great expectation?
- Am I righteous and in right tune with God?

MR. PRAYER MAN, THESE ARE FACTORS THAT CAN HINDER YOUR PRAYERS

- Sin
- Unbelief
- Spiritual indiscipline
- Worldliness and unrighteousness
- Lack of holy spirit baptism
- Weariness in prayers
- Spiritual ignorance

Prayers to help your brain

In Christ is the wisdom of God to man. If any man does not have him, that man has no wisdom. Jesus is the way, truth and life, you cannot associate with the highest thinker except through him.

Do you want to receive him? Pray then with me!

Lord Jesus, I come before you today, I recognize that I am a sinner. Forgive me, come into my life and take total control in Jesus name. Amen!

Now that you have received him, pray your way into becoming a genius:

1. O lord, upgrade my brain by your power.
2. Ministry of head attackers against my brain, expire.
3. Holy Spirit, anoint my creative faculty.
4. Supernatural wisdom, incubate my life.
5. Inherited brain bondage, be broken.
6. Anointing of God, fall upon my brain.
7. O Lord, turn me into a genius.
8. Head attackers, scatter.
9. Praises.

REFERENCES

- Napoleon Hill. *Think and Grow Rich.* 1938. The Ralston Society. Meriden.
- Shiv Khera, *You Can Win.*
- William Atkinson. Thought Vibrations
- Ernest Holmes. *The Science of the Mind.* E-book.
- Tom Corley. *Rich habits: The Secret of Wealthy People.* E-book.
- Tom Corley, *Reinvent Yourself in 30days.* E-book.
- Berridge, KC (2004). *Motivation concepts in behavioral neuroscience. Physiology & Behavior.* **8** *(2): 179–209.* doi:*10.1016/j.physbeh.2004.02.004.* PMID *15159167.*
- Tom Corley. *Brain Science: The Physiology Behind Success and Wealth Creation.* 2014. Online at http://richhabits.net/
- www.sleepora.com/sleepblog

M.I. Bello

www.ingramcontent.com/pod-product-compliance
Lightning Source LLC
Chambersburg PA
CBHW051345040426
42453CB00007B/421